DIALOGUES
AND
IDEOLOGUES

DIALOGUES
AND
IDEOLOGUES

Thomas Molnar

FRANCISCAN HERALD PRESS
1434 West 51st Street   Chicago, Illinois 60609

Dialogues and Ideologues by Thomas Molnar, was first published as *Ecumenism or New Reformation?* in 1968 by Funk & Wagnalls. New edition copyright ©1977 by Franciscan Herald Press, 1434 West 51st Street, Chicago, Illinois 60609. Reprinted with permission of the author and publisher.

Library of Congress Cataloging in Publication Data:

Molnar, Thomas Steven.
   Dialogues and ideologues.

   Edition of 1968 published under title: Ecumenism or new reformation.
   Includes bibliographical references and index.
   1. Church renewal—Catholic Church. 2. Catholic Church—History—20th century. I. Title.
BX1746.M64 1977   262'.001   77-24084
ISBN 0-8199-0679-4

Nihil Obstat:
   MARK P. HEGENER O.F.M.
   Censor Deputatus

Imprimatur:
   MSGR. RICHARD A. ROSEMEYER, J.C.D.
   Vicar General, Archdiocese of Chicago

May 25, 1977

To the memory of my mother

In our age . . . it requires no little courage to say a word to the triumphators of the mob, courage to talk *against the reformers.*

—Sören Kierkegaard,
On Authority and Revelation

Instead of asserting their ideas these Catholics take the ideas of others. They do not convert but let themselves be converted. We have here the reverse phenomenon of the apostolate. We do not conquer but surrender. Surrender is veiled by a whole language, a whole phraseology. Old friends who have remained on the right path are considered reactionaries, traitors. Only those are considered good Catholics who are capable of all the weaknesses, and of all the compromises.

—Monsignor Montini, September 4, 1956

Contents

I

THE CRISIS

There were times, not long ago, when on meeting a priest or a religious on the street or at other occasions, I felt an in-instinctive respect and reverence as one has in the presence of natural superiors. This was not only my experience, it was shared by millions of Catholics, and even by non-Catholics. One hears today testimonies by Protestants, Jews, and adherents of other faiths, according to which the whole world used to consider, and liked to consider, the Roman Church as a rock, the immutably fix point in the turmoil of centuries. A rock, let us add, both in its institutional aspects—although these were subject to change throughout the ages—and in her teaching of the truth she has held uninterruptedly since Christ gave her a mission among men. Writes an Anglican to the London *Times* (January 7, 1967),

> If Rome too were to succumb to doubt, it would lose its attraction. It is Rome's attachment to the ancient faith when around it everything collapses, which is its force. . . .

My respect for the Church of Rome depends on her loyalty to saints and martyrs. Any weakening of this loyalty in the name of ecumenism or of modern ideas would show that Rome too got infected with the Protestant disease.

The letter shows a clear mind and considerable courage. For today it is not fashionable to refer to the Church as a fix point, keeper of the Truth. On the contrary, what is stressed and what is demanded of the Church is that it should evolve, commit itself to change and changing choices even in matters of dogma and doctrine, to be immersed in the world, and participate in remaking society. One hears these demands from all corners, from inside as well as from outside the Church. The quest for reform inside the Church goes back to several decades, and those with a reformist tendency are numerous among theologians, priests, and laymen. They hold that Catholics, and the clergy in particular, lived for centuries a sheltered life in a kind of ghetto; that they were attached to an oldfashioned worldview, translated into attitudes of selfishness, otherworldliness, indifference to real (i.e., social and scientific) problems; that they thought they were apolitical, concerned only with passing through this Valley of Tears, when, in reality, they were on the conservative side of the social barricade, in symbiosis with the powerful. Of masses, poverty, real problems they knew hardly anything, and what they did know never softened their hearts, since they preached resignation to this world and rewards only in the next.

This is going to be drastically changed now—the popular homily runs. Under the impact of tremendous new forces: technology, socialism, ripeness of the world for unity, and mankind's awakening to a common consciousness—we witness the kneading of a new dough, of a new world. This world tolerates no ghettos, not even self-imposed ones: the priests, nuns, and other religious must come out from behind their walls where renunciation and privileges were combined in an unhealthy way of life. The Gospel must become social because men are irresistibly advancing toward a future of economic and cultural equality. Men of good will brook no separating walls, all want to share a sense of community. The "new priest," therefore, must shed the distinguishing signs, live like other people, for only then can the Church hope to preserve contact with the masses of men. Dogmas, tradition, special discipline may survive for a while, but only because they are becoming fast irrelevant. They are expected to fade away with the rest. The emerging Church will teach a demythologized faith, and will display fewer special traits such as institutions, pomp, and ceremony.

Whatever may be the relevance of charges, they do point to a crisis in the Church. The causes of this crisis lie, however, much deeper, and the "inadaptation" to the world is much more fundamental than these charges indicate. The inadaptation is a legacy of Christ, underlined by Saint Paul, Saint Augustine, and every one of the Church Fathers, saints, theologians, and philosophers: *Nolite conformari huic saeculo* ("Do not adopt the ways of the world"), judge them—and also your own actions—by a Christian norm, dare oppose them even at the cost of your life.

The burden of this legacy is manifest in the following way: some hold that this assignment splits the Christian in two parts, as it were, by dividing his loyalties between Caesar and God. Already the pagan Romans accused the Christians of disloyalty to the State since they refused to adore the inanimate as well as the living idols, the mythological deities, and the emperor. Later, from Machiavelli to Rousseau and today's intellectuals, the old accusation was expressed in new terms: the Christian, seeking salvation, develops only individual virtues even if they clash with the needs of the community.

These charges are historically untrue. The Church has always been, by the nature of her mission, a dynamic organization, present in every corner of the earth. In the Roman Empire the Christian was a good and loyal citizen:

He was not "the citizen of the world" nor "the Friend of Man" of the Stoic ideal; he was a plain person who gave himself up for other people, cared for the sick and the

worthless, had a word of friendship and hope for the sinful
and despised, would not go and see men killed in the am-
phitheatre, and—most curious of all—was careful to have
indigent brothers taught trades by which they could help
themselves.[1]

Then in the fifth, sixth, and seventh centuries the Church
took up the burden laid down by the dying Roman Empire to
civilize the barbarians; she taught men, refrained their cruelest
instincts, replaced their primitive laws with a superior legal system, established universities, sponsored the arts, provided a language and unified moral concepts for the western world.

With the beginning of European expansion to other con-
tinents, the Church sent out her missionaries, although, had
she been as selfish as her detractors claim, she would have con-
centrated all her efforts and best talents on combating Protestantism in Europe. Rightly, however, the Church considered
from the beginning that the Europeanization of the world should
also mean the spreading of Christ's message among Indians,
Chinese, the Blacks of Africa, the Polynesians of the Pacific islands. Some individual priests certainly participated in the
worldly spoils on the side of discoverers and conquistadores; but
by far the essential thrust was in the direction of permeating
these non-European environments with the Christian message
of the dignity of the person and with all the practical consequences that follow. It is now fashionable to say that instead of
adapting herself to the mentality and the mores of the native
populations, the Church sought to implant European ways and
ideas among them; yet, I think that Jean de Fabregues is correct
in writing that, in any event, not Europe fashioned Christianity
but, on the contrary, the Church gave Europe her civilizational
forms. In other words, Europe (and the West) bears the imprint
of Christianity; the westernization of the world carried this imprint farther.

The tangible result of the Church's presence in the world

[1] T. R. Glover, *The Conflict of Religions in the Early Roman Empire*
(London, Methuen & Co., 1909; Boston, Beacon Press paperback, 1960).

is not a disaffection of Christians from worldly affairs, but, on the contrary, their eminent contribution to the building of solid social forms: needed institutions, improved methods, a dynamic outlook on life. My own observations in Africa, Asia, and Latin America have convinced me that the best citizens are formed by Christian mission schools and universities, and that Christian charity in instances too many to count overcomes local apathy, inertia, and fatalism, or simply the oppressiveness of the climate. Volumes could be written of the missionaries', priests', and nuns' extraordinary devotion under extremely hard conditions. This devotion, while springing from spiritual founts, shapes and improves people's material wellbeing through schools, hospitals, homes for orphans, the aged, the refugees, the unwed mothers. Whether in Islamic, Buddhist, or Animist lands, in the African jungle, the Bolivian high plateau, and in East Asian refugee centers, the Catholic missionary is almost the only person with both spiritual *and* practical preoccupations, acting like a lifegiving force in a usually inert milieu.

Christ's teaching that man belongs simultaneously to two worlds does not detract his available energies from worldly pursuits; on the contrary, it generates such energies and provides them with spiritual justification for constructive action in the world. It is materialism, specifically Marxism in our time, which deprives man of this justification (that is, of his soul), and weakens in him the concern for others since in the materialistic view man is merely a "force of production."

These arguments, however cogent and verifiable by the objective inquirer, do not convince the opponents of Christianity who consider it an antisocial force. Christ's legacy to which I referred above, the distinction between God's and Caesar's domains, is a scandal for the monists in whose eyes man is one with nature and man's single vocation is to turn his attention entirely to earthly matters. In the view of these critics of Christianity the imperfection of the world is a permanent scandal worsened by Christianity which raised high hopes without fulfilling them. Thus from the very beginning, the Church had to face in various forms the one accusation that her very univer-

sality makes the scandal of evil even more intolerable since the
diffusion of her message did not abolish misery and suffering
among men. Churchmen raise these charges as frequently
today as outright opponents of Christianity. A high prelate
in Recife, Brazil, told me that had Karl Marx found a world
permeated by the Church's love and charity, a Church relieving
slum conditions, drunkenness, and prostitution, he would never
have formulated his theories and doctrines. I had no success in
reminding him that most enemies of the Church attack her because they deny the *doctrinal* validity of Christ's teachings.

It is time now to give concrete illustrations of the crisis
through which the Church is passing. The examples I selected
show that we cannot dismiss the crisis as resulting from partial
discontent with some specific abuse or from a sudden need of
emancipation leading to minor and understandable excesses. In
other words, what is now in question is not *reform* but *Reformation,* a conscious and willed effort to transform the Church
doctrinally, morally, and structurally. It is ironic that Father
Yves Congar wrote less than two decades ago that the reform-
minded Catholics today are not at all like the rebellious modern-
ists of the last century: they are respectful of the Church and
favor changes without questioning authority and doctrine. They
display neither radicalism nor impatience, which would be signs,
according to Father Congar, of "false reformism." [2] Yet, one
wonders whether Congar's diagnosis is correct and his hopes
warranted. The examples which follow show conclusively that
the reformist movement has got out of control. Indeed, Jacques
Maritain seems directly to contradict the above passage when he
writes, fifteen years and a Council later, of the "neo-modernist
fever . . . in the so-called 'intellectual' circles, compared to
which the modernism of the time of Pius X was only a modest
hay fever." [3]

The structural crisis. A particularly vicious scandal going
deeper than a mere historical controversy has been the one rag-

[2] *Vraie et fausse réforme dans l'Eglise* (Paris, Editions du Seuil, 1950),
pp. 40, 570.
[3] *Le Paysan de la Garonne* (Paris, Desclée de Brouwer, 1966), p. 16.

ing around the personality and policies of Pope Pius XII. On the surface the matter appears to affect the Vatican's wartime attitude regarding Hitlerism and the persecution of Jews in national-socialist Germany. We must briefly examine this surface the better to understand the technique of how *one* level is exploited for the purposes of another on which the battle lines are joined.

It is held that Pius XII, already pro-German in his years as Papal Nuncio in Munich, became a Nazi-sympathizer during the Hitler years, and refused to raise his voice against Jewish persecutions, including the gassing of millions at Auschwitz. It is further argued that the Vatican was willing to sacrifice the Jews so as not to hinder Hitler's war efforts which were directed essentially at fighting bolshevism.

What emerges from these charges is less the historic figure of Pius than a straw-man Pope who, like a scapegoat, is burdened with all the sins of an office, the papacy, stumbling block for Protestants and repository of "authoritarianism" in the eyes of various ideologues. Pieced together from Rolf Hochhuth's play, *The Deputy*, from books by Saul Friedlander, Jacques Nobécourt, and others, we see Pius as aristocratic and authoritarian, intelligent but cold, uncharitable as a diplomat of *Realpolitik*, above all closed to the generous aspirations of his time, whether to heretical teachings or to a thawing and softening communism.

Vatican historians, with the records of the Vatican archives, of the German Foreign Office and Allied Governments at their disposal, have now refuted conclusively all the allegations of the above writers. They showed that Pius did a great deal for the Jews, and went to the limit of what was feasible in the teeth of a brutal ideology and its exterminating machine.[4] Yet, the purpose of the detractors was not at all the clearing up of the record, but the attack on the papacy itself. Pius XII is

---

[4] It is never mentioned, for example, that deeply affected by Pius' wartime role, a Roman rabbi, Zarelli, became a Catholic after the war. On the whole controversy, see the objective and courageous analysis of Alexis Curvers, "Pie XII et les faux témoins," *Itinéraires*, November 1965.

singled out because of his strong personality and the intellectual precision and vigor with which he stood as a rampart against the introduction of the world's confusion into the Church. A sort of ritual persecution has been performed on his memory because it is felt that in his person the very principle of Peter's authority and the continuity of the Church can be undermined. With the Pope's position rendered problematic, the bishop's authority may also be questioned and freedom of worship and doctrine introduced.

The Jewish question is used by enemies of Pius in order to place him in the rank of Hitler's secret partisans, thereby to discredit him in the most scandalous way. This interpretation is the more plausible as nobody seems to draw the obvious parallels from Pius' "failure" to sacrifice his own person in the gas chambers, and his as well as his successors' (John and Paul) "failure" to go to Vorkuta and Karaganda, or any of the other Soviet concentration camps, offering their person to persecution and imprisonment, a testimony for Christ among the wretched. Yet nobody ever mentions this second failure because the desired thesis is meant to differentiate sharply between Pius and his successors as symbols, respectively, of the "old" and "new" Church. It is now common to place Pius XII, at least by indirection, next to Stalin among the fossils of a bygone age when totalitarian systems—the Catholic Church before the Council and the Soviet Union before its "liberalization"—nurtured brutal and wily despots, surrounding them with a personality cult. This gross method serves for drawing a sharp dividing line between pre- and post-conciliar Church; the attack against the pope is designed to weaken the Church in the center of her institutional life, and the attack is launched precisely by those who recommend strong centralization in the life of the political community. Obviously, they intend to dissolve the former's structure by introducing democracy (in the guise of "episcopal collegiality"), and strengthen the latter by pulling all threads together in the hands of centralized governments.

This is a dangerous procedure at a time when political bodies almost everywhere are impregnated by aggressive ideologies. The bishops of a national Church can resist less efficiently than the distant and independent papacy to their respective governments. The threat is more than evident in Communist and other totalitarian countries where governmental efforts are directed at the severance of ties between their Catholic citizens and the Vatican. The pressure on bishops and faithful is easily stepped up until it becomes unbearable as it was demonstrated in Communist China, but also in Hitler's Germany, Tito's Yugoslavia, Castro's Cuba, and elsewhere. But even outside the totalitarian orbit the signs are ominous; in the United States one may wonder how long the Catholic bishops would be able to withstand pressure (not by the government so much as by public opinion and the pressure groups) to liberalize birth control, abortion, or other such legislation if they were alone, without the firmness of the Vatican backing them.

Yet, this is the essential orientation of the recommended structural changes. Some of their outward signs are: the obligatory retirement of prelates above the age of seventy-five (will this rule apply to popes too, one wonders?); the general weakening of the Curia, reputedly the hotbed of conservatism; the automatic resignation of the curial cardinals at the death of each pope; and the establishment of a permanent synod not merely to assist the pope but to act as a deliberative chamber. All this is, of course, the preparation of a democratic structure for the Church—at a time when parliamentary democracy shows signs of senility, inefficiency, and general eclipse. But again: what from the outside appears as the structural reform of an institution, in reality aims at the weakening of papal authority before various pressure groups. True, the historical argument for the change is that the early churches, founded in all parts of the Roman Empire, were equal among themselves and not subordinated to Rome; why not restore the initial situation and make the National Conferences of Bishops co-governing bodies with the papal administration?

The Church, however, is not only a historical body, but it is also, and primarily, the creation of faith. As such, it is not simply a local church that was founded in Jerusalem on the day of

Pentecost; it is the universal Church that the Holy Spirit in-
structs. Before even one local church was founded, the Apostles
were in communion with Peter to whom Christ had said: "You
are Peter, and on this rock I will build my Church." *This*
Church, around Peter, contained the seeds of all the other
churches that were to be founded.

The moral crisis. What goals are pursued by those who
keep the so-called "celibacy issue" alive? Most ordinary Catholics, the laity whom the ecclesiastics are supposed now to consult
as equals, find the idea of married priests repugnant. The medieval Church declared against a married clergy because of the
abuses to which it gave rise, but primarily because a Roman
priest must have only one worldly concern: his parish, his pupils,
his sick, his missionary colony. A wife, children, and family
would not only put the weight of his preoccupations elsewhere,
but also would make him more timid in these times of persecution: his first concern would be like that of many Protestant
clergymen in Hitlerist Germany and Communist China, the
safety of his family, with his sacerdotal tasks a poor second.

The related requirement is, of course, chastity. Not only
was this Christ's example and Paul's preferred status, but those
who would so lightly abolish celibacy conveniently forget that
the young priest looking forward to marriage would have to pass
through the experience of courtship and methods of mate-
selection prevailing in his society. In our western societies this
would mean that the future priest (and nun) would partake of
premarital sexual practices that are expected of all others. In
fact, there is already at least one priest who advertises in sex-
scandal sheets his hopes that the Church will legalize the so-
called "trial-marriages" between youngsters!

But let us grant, with some Machiavellian minds, that celibacy would be made elective. That those who are "not made
for it" would choose the married state; that only the secular
clergy might marry, but not the regular one. And so on, possibly
ad infinitum, variations are offered on the theme of sex—the net
effect of which is to introduce division in the Church at vital
seams of its fabric.

Beyond the pseudo-learned studies on celibacy and beyond the sensational polls of priests about their preference, one must point to the documented relationship between the various heresies and sexual license. The celibacy issue does not stand as an isolated topic among today's critical problems; it must be seen as part, a central part, of the changed outlook on sexual morality that intellectuals within the Church are trying to accredit. The objective is to put the *homo naturalis* in the place of the *homo religiosus* and to show that the essence of the former is sexual freedom, while the essence of the latter is "love." Sexual freedom is not in need of subtle definitions but "love" can be surrounded with an aura of vagueness which authorizes man and woman to do as they please. An example of this is the recent statement of the British Council of Churches which consisted of embarrassed, wishy-washy, yet clear enough neo-pagan admissions that all sexual acts in whatever situation are licit, including perversions if privately indulged in. Another group, British Quakers (as reported by Father Richard A. McCormick in *The Catholic World*), refuses to condemn premarital and even homosexual relations in the name of love. "Where there is genuine tenderness, an openness to responsibility and the seed of commitment, God is surely not shut out," their statement runs.

Less embarrassed and more vulgar is Father Marc Oraison, French priest-psychoanalyst, who considers the Church's entire concept of sexual sin to be out of date, physically as well as morally. He calls for the acceptance of masturbation in adolescents as an act similar to and not more serious than the infant's thumb sucking. Both are autoerotic manifestations, he writes.

All this is evidently an immensely unwarranted extension of Augustine's dictum: "Love, and do as you wish." Heretics, with various pretexts, began or ended with unbridled sexual permissiveness. Usually they did so with a detour: considering themselves "elect," that is "pure," they declared that no sin could iconoclastic fury (a kind of spiritual *furor teutonica*) has made ownership of women, the keeping of concubines were not only accepted among them, but were indeed required proof that sin did not soil them. Sexual excesses were thus the very sign of

saintliness, whether among certain medieval sects, the followers
of Thomas Münzer, or the Pietists of the eighteenth century.

Jacques Maritain speaks of this aspect of Luther's movement in his *Three Reformers*. He points out the relationship
between the doctrine that considers man abysmally sinful
through original sin, and the justification of sexuality. There is
indeed a strange and subtle relationship here: man whom Luther considers totally sinful and abandoned by God, will seek,
motivated by a mixture of revenge for God's aloofness and the
consequent permissiveness, an unbridled sexual license. This is
why the contemporary doubt about the very existence of God
communicates itself to so-far decent living members of the
Church as an invitation to begin doing the opposite. Since ab-
stention from sex is the most forceful symbol of commitment to
God, the weakening of belief does not lead progressively to immorality but unleashes it instantly. "Just as it is not within my
power not to be a man, it does not depend on me that I cannot
live without a woman," declared Luther with brutal simplicity.
Maritain comments:

> Unleashing sexuality everywhere under the pretext of re-
> moving intolerable burdens and making virtue easier to
> practise, Luther exhorts the nuns to look for husbands on
> an ignoble tone. . . . Few spectacles were more shameless
> than what carnal frenzy offered in Germany. Religious of
> both sexes, unbound by Luther, were only looking for op-
> portunities to detach themselves from the Church, like
> gangrened limbs from the body.[5]

One can rather easily observe these days, too, the rapid rise
of sexuality to the surface of most movements designed to "renew" the Church. Coeducational seminaries, offensively dressed
priests, charm courses for nuns, the public discussion by both of
psychological problems arising from sexual repression, the indis-
criminate mixing of ecclesiastics with crowds of the least inhib-
ited—it is easy to understand that these are channels through

[5] *Les Trois Réformateurs* (Paris, Editions Plon, 1925), pp. 262.

which the senses may be provoked and the boundary line between licit and illicit erased. Indeed, what more dubious situation can one imagine than the "experiment" at Cuernavaca where the Benedictine abbot, Gregoire Lemercier, had his sixty monks psychoanalyzed by an atheist woman; at the end forty of the monks discovered that they lacked vocation and left the monastery.

The doctrinal crisis. One might say that the two illustrations of the crisis described above are somewhat peripheral to doctrine. But one of the objectives of this book is to show that the crisis in the Church is like crises in any organization: internal weakening and external assault go together; when the first becomes obvious, the second manifests itself on all fronts, so that corruption reaches the center simultaneously with the margins. Only the superficial observer will state that the process has started from incidental causes and then spread in depth.

The year 1517 was clearly not the beginning of the Reformation; it had begun centuries earlier with Marsilius of Padua and William Occam.[6] These men, as well as others, had questioned fundamental doctrine, and their questions reechoed throughout the fifteenth century. Luther's Roman voyage, the controversy over the indulgences, even the Wittemberg theses, were signs on the surface, made possible by the existence of much deeper doubts and more violent disagreements.

The same is true about the present dispute over *transsubstantiation*. Press reports ask, partly in ignorance, partly in pretended surprise, why would such an issue, obscure and "medieval" as it is, agitate modern minds at all? Some people recall the date of the Council of Trent when this controversy was settled, and express the opinion that a scientific age cannot possibly

---

[6] "The results of Occamism and nominalism," writes Father Congar, "were these: consciences became shaken, the certitudes concerning the Church's structure, the role and powers of the hierarchy started to dissolve; there began the dissociation between the institutional Church and a pure Church of the true faithful; the theology of the sacraments was questioned; and people showed inability to think of the Church as a sacramental organism." *Op. cit.*, p. 375.

be interested in arguments of such a nature. Yet a very momen-
tous issue is involved, and its significance is not lost on many
minds. Those who attack this dogma know well why they do so.
The encyclical *Humani Generis* (1950) spoke of them in these
terms:

> There are those who hold that the doctrine of transsubstan-
> tiation is based on a philosophically dated notion of the
> substance, and that it must now be corrected. That the real
> presence of Christ in the Eucharist should be reduced to a
> symbolic presence, still spiritually efficacious.

Paul VI, in turn, wrote the encyclical *Mysterium Fidei*
(1966) in order to reassert the truth in this matter, a truth dis-
puted, although still indirectly, by certain Dutch Catholic circles as well as others, less clearly identifiable. They interpret this
central mystery of the faith under the label: *transsignification*
(also: *transfinalization*).

Why is this a central issue? The claim of Christian superiority over all other religions rests on three pillars: that it is a
religion of love; that its factualness is historically demonstrated;
and that it begins with God's Incarnation. Christianity does not
have a prophet like Moses or Mohammed who receives the Revelation from God and communicates it to men; Christianity's
central figure *is* Christ the God who became man in order to
save us by his unique act of sacrifice. Christianity would be a
religion like any other without the Incarnation, and without
Christ's promise that He will be really, existentially present in
the offering of the Mass.

When a group of Catholics interprets this promise and this
presence as merely symbolic or metaphorical, it makes of the
Mass a simple anniversary celebration and empties it of all mystery and truth. It may still be a solemn event, but one which
represents different things to different people, like any ceremony
where the externals count more than the content. Understandably, the existential link is then severed with the living God, and
the door opens for further dissolution of the remaining link
through "demythologization" of the Nativity and paschal his-

tory. Not to speak of the doubt thus cast on Christ's promise: This is my body and this is my blood.[7.]

The Dutch Catholic intellectuals and their more or less vocal supporters elsewhere argue with the help of questionable subtleties. But as behind so many critical issues, the intellectuals' argument here too is that the scientifically emancipated man of our age cannot accept the too farfetched chemistry of transsubstantiation. A symbolic meaning of the act is closer to the modern mind. In later passages of this book I will have to return to the controversy of what the modern mind can or cannot accept; however, this is a good place to examine briefly the basis of the charges that the Church (and other religions too, for that matter) is anthropomorphic, that it conceives God with human features and attributes.

The transsubstantiation debate means that we, modern men, should cease thinking of God on such a human pattern. In this particular debate the argument is that the Mass is a refined reenactment of primitive man's cannibalistic ceremony when he eats the flesh and drinks the blood of admired beings, whether animal or human, so as to absorb the envied characteristics. In the course of the history of cannibalism which, incidentally, has not yet ended as recent examples showed, such "diet" consisted of the body of fallen animals, protective of the clan or threatening it, of slaughtered enemies, and also of old members of the clan who, when deceased or ritually murdered, could communicate to the young their wisdom, if no longer their physical vigor.

We show a strange contempt for our ancestors when we assume that only with a primitive mentality can one envision the presence of a superior force in the food we absorb. Since the practice is universal in time and space, there is no contradiction

---

[7] This is what Bishop Bossuet wrote about the controversy in the seventeenth century: "If we had preserved the correct and natural meaning of the words: 'This is my body, this is my blood,' we would think we explained sufficiently the real presence of Jesus Christ in the Eucharist. But since many wish to mean that Jesus Christ was present only figuratively, spiritually, or by his virtue or faith, then, to avoid ambiguity, it was believed better to say that Our Lord's body was really and substantially present. This is how the term transsubstantiation was born." *History of the Variations of the Protestant Churches*, Bk. 3, Ch. 16.

in suggesting that men have always believed that they could communicate with these superior forces, either through oral absorption or oral prayers. If God can *hear* my prayer, He can also be present in the bread and wine I consume.

Cannibalism has always been practiced in places where other foods also abounded, in Africa, South America, the tropical islands, etc. Thus the eating of human flesh was not motivated by scarcity or by the particularly good taste of this flesh, but by religious beliefs. Obscurely, men wanted to communicate with superior forces or with beings who had become superior through death. And, after all, we too witness everyday the transformation of food into blood, fat, hormones and energy (metabolism). So that if the proponents of "transsignification" deny the Real Presence of Christ in the offering of the Mass, this is not because they question the possibility of one substance changing into another, but because they question the Divinity of Christ and his Incarnation.[8] They do not hesitate to accept the hypothesis of evolutionary mutation or the transformation of elements under nuclear bombardment. The scandal in their eyes is something else.

It is, first, the Church's insistence that God is not merely an abstract moral norm, a blind force, or an esthetic ideal, but a reality in our existence. The abstraction-seeking mind of many intellectuals believes that it has refined a concept when it has only made it pale and inaccessible to the senses. Already a Greek philosopher mocked the pious for personifying their gods, and added that if cattle had gods they would picture them under bovine aspects. Our contemporary philosophers (like the Dutch Catholic group) argue in the same manner.

But, we ask, what is wrong in all this? Man is a being of reason, emotions, and imagination; and he needs all three to

[8] In this they follow the Arian heretics of the fourth and fifth centuries. Writes Jean Guitton: "Arius felt strongly about the inaccessibility of God. This feeling, again strong in our times, is based on the idea that God is conceived as above everything, above existence itself. . . . Such a doctrine, when applied thoroughly, would make God unthinkable, would destroy the idea of divine fatherhood and the habit of prayer." *Le Christ écartelé* (Paris, Librairie Académique Perrin, 1963), p. 124.

have a better grasp of God who challenges his depth. For my part, I find it infinitely moving when people set their imagination to work at their idea of God. The cannibal's obscure concept of a superior being approaches him, or an Italian peasant's familiarity with the saints show groping yet true insights. If contemporary Protestantism—but not yet the Catholics and the Greco-Orthodox—has become so disincarnated and unmoored from the foundations, it is because the Protestants' iconoclastic fury (a kind of spiritual *furor teutonica*) has made it ever more difficult for them to form real relationships with the living God.

The second scandal follows from the first: with their depersonalized concept of God, the proponents of a revision of the dogma of transsubstantiation find it unbearable that history might not be an impersonal concatenation of mechanical or evolutionary motions but a dialogue of God with men, at times reaching a dramatic climax. As it did in the reign of Tiberius Caesar, under Pontius Pilate's governorship in Judea.

II

NEW AND OLD
CRITICS

The present crisis in the Church is the result of a certain number of clearly perceivable causes. But to a large and dangerous extent confusion about these causes is created and maintained by the character of the means through which social, political, and intellectual groups communicate with each other in our age. The means, the "media" of communications, over-simplify complex issues, focus on the present with the virtual exclusion of the past, and are owned and managed by interest groups with an antispiritual ideology. Thus the degree of confusion is heightened by the structure of information-carrying.

This is not to say that the crisis is only a matter of "lack of communication." Reporters, commentators, publicists, and news agencies are, naturally, committed to the presentation of events with a news value, and are, therefore, inclined to write up sensational stories about everyday events. But not even their predisposition and their art can create something out of nothing; they shout "fire in the Church" because the smoke is indeed visible behind her walls.

The communications media, as well as the mentality and psychological inclinations of our societies which these media exploit, are responsible for the widespread, perhaps even general belief that the present crisis in the Church is something entirely new and also decisive for the future. In the superficial observer's view our age appears as cataclysmic; everybody has the word "revolution" on his lips, and one easily imagines in this highstrung atmosphere that the old world is cracking up and a new one is aborn. One concludes that religion, the faith, the Church are disappearing or, at least, are undergoing such enormous transformations (the fashionable term is "mutation" with its biological connotation, meaning that the transformation is necessary and not subject to divine or human control) that the outcome will be unrecognizable. Hence the multiplication of prophets and forecasters who speak of a "new Church."

The impression is reinforced by the actual changes in style of life which give rise to a general conviction that nothing like this happened before. Since we now tend to ignore the past (in education, family tradition, art, etc.), the average man, living in a vacuum of comparisons and unsupported by past examples, becomes rapidly persuaded that he is witnessing unique events when, in reality, he witnesses a repetition of old conflicts, charges, and complaints. He may like or dislike what he witnesses, but with the *present* drumming on his ears, he accepts his isolation from earlier-held beliefs and surrenders, defenseless, to spokesmen for an imaginary future.

Thus the crisis in the Church is apprehended by most people as isolated but multiplying instances of baffling words and events. Although the crisis has reached amazing proportions, most Catholics, and also non-Catholics, ask themselves what is happening around them. Their eyes fall on this or that strange occurrence, but they are unable to correlate these occurrences. Thus they experience the crisis as an increasingly acute malaise, but only a malaise without analysis and critical awareness. Meanwhile those who cause it and exploit it, namely, the Church intellectuals, move on the inside tracks, and their enterprise is coordinated by publications, magazines, books, public discussions, and so on.

Our first task in this book is, then, to help the reader correlate the seemingly isolated cases and show that an internal logic links them to one another.

The second task is to list instances of the crisis and relate them with the past, particularly, of course, with Church history. The immediate benefit of this double operation is that we become less alarmed: for next to our unshakable faith that the Church possesses the divine promise is the historical experience of other crises, successfully surmounted. This should not lead either to fatalism or complacency: any alarm signal in the Church must be taken with extreme seriousness; heresies, although they will accompany the Church to the end of time, must be combated and cured. But the knowledge that similar events took place before helps us regain a much-needed perspective.

Every heresy in the Church begins by the assertion of one man or of a group that they are the repositories of true knowledge (*gnosis*), and that all previous affirmations of theologians, popes, and philosophers are based on falseness and error. The "gnostic" group then proceeds not to reform the Church according to its own light although in harmony with tradition, but to rebuild her after a perfect blueprint. With the impatience of utopians, also with the utopians' disrespect for what exists and for organically grown tradition, they set about with simpleminded enthusiasm to demolish the old and construct the new. The mentality is illustrated by a text in *Commonweal*.

What justifies the Church's doctrines, traditions and structures? To ask such questions is, in a vital sense, to begin all over, to ask with utter courage and an uncompromising desire for truth why the Church exists and whether it should go on existing.

We witness this movement today with its full-blown impatience and disrespect, also with its limitless belief in having

found the formula for perfection. Earlier heretics began by criti-
cizing the Church for having gone astray at a certain point of
her history and concluded that everything was evil in her and
that she needed to be radically reconstructed. Since preoccupation with history, its dates and records, was not in the
forefront of preoccupations, these earlier heretics did not engage
in historical research in the modern sense; they satisfied themselves by denouncing the corruption which they considered as
Satan's usurpation of the papal throne; then they proceeded to
proclaim their own truth, their own illumination, the true
Church.

The partisans of the new movement make the following
analysis of the crisis in the Church, an analysis in which their
insistence on "dialogue" and "updating" is at once evident. Today's potential heretics pay more attention to historical detail.
They refer to the Reformation and hold that Luther, Calvin,
Zwingli, Münzer, John Knox were men disillusioned with the un-
yielding stubbornness of the Roman Church, or rather, a majority in the Roman Church. There was, they say, a minority in and
around the Vatican which understood the grievances of the
would-be Reformers, and favored, in fact, a refashioned Church.
What took place instead was the victory of the intolerant "right
wing"; the bitterness was allowed to spread in Christendom, and
the Council of Trent definitively slammed the door on compromise. Since 1563 Rome has been on the defensive, has allowed
its position to become increasingly rigid, as if Christ's teaching
were a miser's treasure to be defended against outsiders.

The consequence of this rift, so the argument continues,
was that the modern world emerged largely apart from the Roman Church, under Protestant secularist inspiration. The formulators of science, secular philosophy, socially enlightened views:
Descartes, Galileo, Voltaire, Rousseau, later Kant, Hegel, Marx,
Darwin, and Freud, wrote and otherwise exerted their influence
outside if not against the Church, with Catholics merely as by-
standers, either self-righteous or vaguely worried. Thus since the
sixteenth century, then at an accelerated rate since the French
Revolution, the world became successively republican, liberal.

democratic, industrialized, Marxist, scientific, technological, and so on, while the Church grew increasingly detached from these realities, indeed reacted to them in a censorious way from the Galileo case to the *Syllabus* (1864) and beyond.

But did the Church really oppose progress, scientific and social? It is essential to examine these questions because the whole issue of whether the Church is "open" or "closed" to the world hinges on them in the eyes of her critics. If anything, the Church's stand in the Galileo case has been doubly vindicated. The new, Einsteinian view of the universe reduces the value of Galileo's system to that of a hypothesis, one of many possible ways of looking at the phenomena in question. The Church authorities never asked more of the great astronomer than just this recognition. Cardinal Barberini, the future Pope Urban VIII, insisted that before the Copernican system might be accepted as true in the Galilean sense, it would be necessary to demonstrate not only that it accounted for all phenomena, but also "that the whole thing cannot, without involving contradiction, be accounted for by any system other than the one you have conceived." He advised Galileo to present his Copernican views as mathematically convenient hypotheses rather than as established truth about reality.[1] An advice that twentieth-century critics, committed to the evolutionist view, ought to take to heart when they instruct the Church to adapt her doctrine to the theory of evolution. What if *their* view of evolution will seem as unscientific to biologists three hundred years hence, as Pope Urban's and Cardinal Bellarmine's opinions about astronomy seem now to them?

[1] The American philosopher, Morris R. Cohen, writes about this in his *Studies in Philosophy and Science*: "Einstein's later theory of relativity reopens the issue between Galileo and those who condemned him for saying that the earth is in motion. If there is no absolute space and all motion is relative, it is just as true to say that the earth moves with reference to this car is to say that this car moves with reference to the earth." Professor Cohen argues, after Einstein, that it is possible to define a space with regard to which the fixed stars are rotating. In such a space the earth may be considered at rest. (See, for the discussion of the Galileo controversy, *The Achievement of Galileo*, edited by James Brophy and Henry Paolucci (New York, Twayne Publishers, 1962).

The second justification follows from the first: science, whose march throughout the ages consists of an indefinite number of steps adjusting theories to observed phenomena, cannot serve as a criterion for nonscientific phenomena. Matters of faith, of human insights, the religious, artistic, and social domain cannot be broken down into elementary data as Galileo's contemporary, Descartes, proposed, and cannot be measured and experimented with. The danger of submitting everything to scientific analysis, taking physics as the basic science, became first noticeable in the seventeenth century. Machiavelli, a hundred years before Descartes, then Spinoza and Hobbes, suggested the reducibility of every human endeavor to geometrical and physical data which presaged similar efforts with regard to religion too. Savonarola, and more decisively Pascal (another of Galileo's contemporaries), fought this tendency of modern thought. Pascal's conclusion is that the spirit of religion is incommensurable with scientific data and unanswerable to scientific analysis in the Cartesian sense.

Today's critics also hold that the Church failed, since the Reformation, to update herself in other respects too, namely in the matter of social and economic changes. This is why the Vatican Council is hailed by them as not merely an occasion for certain internal reforms, but for a veritable revolution. (The "October Revolution of the Church," as Father Congar expressed it.) In their eyes the *Syllabus*, now a century old although its main tenets were reaffirmed by Pius X at the start of this century, embodies the old reactionary attitude designed to build a barricade against modernistic doctrines. On the other hand, the decrees of the Vatican Council, in particular *Gaudium et Spes* dealing with the modern world, are interpreted as a radically new orientation for the Church: acceptance of the world as it is, especially as it will be according to the interpretation of contemporary scientists, sociologists, psychologists, and others.

The Church is warned that in this emerging world she must abandon the "Constantinian principle" of politicizing her evangelical message which leads to a too-close association with the ruling class. The critics say that the Church was "really" herself, that is, the carrier of Christ's message, only in the first three centuries of her existence, while she was persecuted and suffered martyrdom. When Emperor Constantine adopted Christianity as a State religion and even stood over its first great council, the temptation to profit by the favor of the secular power proved too strong to be resisted. In the next seventeen hundred years the Church successfully linked her destinies with those of the ruling classes whose interests, in turn, she was ready to protect. It followed from this attitude, say the radical critics, that in proportion as socially lower classes are now rebelling against the unjust structure of society, the Church, identified with upper classes and their interests, is also condemned to liquidation or at least radical transformation of its structure. This historical inevitability was not clearly perceived until the last few decades; at present, however, the sociopolitical upheavals following the Second World War are rapidly uncovering the flaws in the edifice; the Church is obliged to give up her long-held positions and attitudes which are definitively discredited. New forces are reshaping the world; the Church may choose to remain immobile and thus to be bypassed by historical evolution, or shed her old crust and renew herself together with a rejuvenated mankind.

Yet if we examine what these critics are saying, we find that they by no means seek charitably to disengage the Church from the clutches of the "Constantinian principle" and free her for purely spiritual attitudes. Rather, they accept the presently fashionable sociohistorical theories about a supposedly emerging classless society, and urge the Church to adapt herself to it. But would this reconversion not be a superficial one, a new application of the Constantinian attitude? The term "classless society" is a convenient label hiding a new power structure; adaptation to it for the Church would mean an alliance with a new power structure, not with a world from which power is at last eliminated. For the critics' entire analysis, which they advertise as a neo-Christian discovery, is based on Marxist theory. When the "last" class, the proletariat, will have overthrown bourgeois capitalism, Marx held, the result will not be a new domination by one class (except for a supposedly brief period of the "dicta-torship of the proletariat") but a classless society. From this society, covering the entire planet, politics will be by definition excluded—if we follow Marx and define "politics" as the differ-ence in the level of power among classes, a difference exploited by the most powerful.

On the other hand, if we assume, and mankind's whole history documents this assumption, that politics is a natural in-gredient of all human communities, then we can only warn against the rush of the Church's critics to involve the Church in a new political relationship, this time with the new holders of power. The fact that the latter do not wear the same distinguish-ing signs of their power and privilege as noblemen of the past should not blind us to the reality of their power and their appe-tite for more power. What is this if not a continuation of the Constantinian principle, with new yet similar actors on both sides? It is hard to see what the difference might be between the Lord Bishop of the eleventh century, acting like any feudal lord, inserted into the worldly hierarchy, a haughty nobleman finding his pleasure in hunting with his retinue of servers—and a con-temporary prelate, attentive to the siren song of the communi-cations media, cultivating his "image" like a politician or a film star, tolerating the jazz-Mass or rock-'n'-roll in the Church, and making demagogic statements about the necessary revolution. Both prelates, the feudal lord and the one engrossed in his own public relations, represent merely two ways of succumbing to the world in the fashion of the day. And let us not believe either that the second type is less "political" than the first; many a time I debated prominent Churchmen in public and observed their desperate even though clumsy way of flattering the pow-ers that be. Not necessarily the public authorities, in case they are on the wane at the time, but with an excellent flair, the vocal and influential pressure groups, tomorrow's public power.

Criticism of the Church and proposals for her radical re-construction sound very modern, indeed, to ears unaccustomed or wilfully deaf to instances of history. Yet, every heretical or perfectionist movement of the past had the same motivations as similar movements have today; they held the same reasoning, made the same leap into unwarranted positions—and died off for the same rootlessness in human nature.

Some illustrations will suffice to establish an exact parallel between the present and various points in Church history. From the start the Church had to assert her views derived from Christ against oriental doctrines which assailed her. The stumbling block was the scandal of evil which persisted although the Church claimed that the Incarnation saved man. Against this claim the critics believed they could legitimately denounce the continued existence of evil. The Jews could at least point out that evil exists because the Messiah had not yet come. But Christians had no such refuge: they seemed to have cornered themselves with their faith in Christ being God who comes among men to remit their sins and show the way to salvation.

Heresies usually began by accusing the Church for being too worldly and authoritarian, that is, impure and full of evil. This was an indication that the Church had never been, or at least had ceased to be, divine or under divine protection. The temptation was therefore strong for many Christians to adopt the Gnostic doctrine as a more satisfactory explanation. It taught that God is not responsible for evil since creation itself is not His work but that of his emanation, the Demiurge. Men too are the creatures of the Demiurge who fashioned them from evil matter fused with sparks of divine light, stolen from God.

This is why men are burdened down through their material side (evil), but also why they aspire to regain unity with God and become perfect. As long as this reunification is not effected men will be miserable, but God too will be less than perfect since parts of his essence went into the fashioning of men. Salvation, according to the Gnostics, would mean that God regains the missing parts when all created men become one with Him. Let us note that in this act of salvation *all* men must participate (not a single particle of light may be missing from the final unity), and that the whole effort, the effort of overcoming matter (evil) rests on man alone, not on God.

Thus the meaning of the Gnostic message is that God is passive, and that man not only saves himself, but in the process he also saves (i.e., restores) God. The conclusion is implicit: man, or rather all men together, mankind, is superior to God, and through relentless activity must count on itself to abolish evil. It is easy to detect the modern variant of this message, the aggressive secularism confident in mankind's ability to bring about paradise on earth without reference to a transcendental absolute. Gnosticism, it is evident, is not merely an old doctrine buried under the ruins of the ancient world. It is an ingenious way of interpreting the essential questions we always will ask about God, man, evil, and the cure of evil. In various guises Gnosticism, combined with other doctrines, has periodically reappeared in the history of the Church, and indeed of the West so decisively influenced by Christianity, up to the present day. Although it is distinct from Manicheism, they usually appear together. Since they both teach that the world of matter (the created world) is evil, they agree that the children of light who harbor a divine soul must progressively disengage themselves from its clutches and constitute a society of the elect, an invisible Church, superior to the one still engulfed in the material world. Thus faith in being an elect is sufficient, and no works or sacraments are needed as the established Christian Churches teach.

Similar were the beliefs of nondenominational Christian sects in the seventeenth century, Anabaptists, Anti-Trinitarians, Dutch Mennonites, Quakers, Quietists, and others. In their narrow framework they set up model religious societies, structureless utopias, in which members were supposed to communicate directly, without social and organizational ties. We see in this the avoidance of worldly involvement, but these societies regularly failed in perpetuating themselves because no human community can exist without a political structure; they either dispersed, or allowed a group of Elect to emerge in their midst.

The Pietists too had contempt for the Church, and hoped to found the real Church among the "regenerated" faithful; the Montanist sect wanted to abolish the authority of the hierarchy and replace it with personal inspiration. With this the Pietists too agreed since they did not believe in the sacraments, only in the illumined internal faith.

Such doctrines, or rather doctrine in the singular since we see that they are variants of a central theme, morbidly enclosed in its self-righteousness, easily shift emphasis and adopt the other extreme. If no institution and tradition watches over those who consider themselves "elect," they remain sole judges of their acts, guided exclusively by their inner (i.e., divine) light. Moreover, the status of Elect preserves them of all sin, and whatever they do, be it immoral by Christian standards, cannot affect their purity. In fact, the more completely they defy these standards, the greater proof they obtain of their own essential purity and innocence, of their having overcome the stains of original sin. From this there is only one step to proclaim oneself untouched by original sin, as the Pelagians taught. Many medieval and other heretics, for example the Montanists, actually said of themselves that they are as pure as Christ, that they *are* Christ.

It is by no means a paradox that as these external forms (sacraments, hierarchy, institutional Church) relaxed, there spread a considerable doctrinal indifference which, in turn, facilitated the multiplication of forms of worship and doctrine. In the case of the Pietists this indifference was masked by piety, and the pretext was that the Elect, the pure-in-heart, needs no doctrine. We see the same thing today. The Church, as shown earlier, is accused of a strict structural authoritarianism, of an inhuman moral stance, and of holding onto doctrines adequate for a more primitive past, but not for man in the age of science. Over against the Church's supposed rigidity, personal and group inspiration is extolled under the labels of "freedom of conscience" and "experimentation." In other words, *democracy* and *science* are the main battering rams against the Church today, exactly as in the past; but democracy was then conceived as the

company of regenerates (or perfect ones, or Elect) who need no .
outward, institutional signs and rely only on their faith; and science was called gnosis, or true knowledge securing salvation. Today, as in the past, religious indifference and experimentation
with worship, liturgy, theology are parallel phenomena because
they demonstrate the weak hold of doctrine and because both
are directed toward a new faith, indeed the foundation of a new
Church.

Today as in the past the restless search for new forms in the
name of personal light encourages the belief that men have
reached maturity and are no longer in need of traditionally conceived religion. Montanus taught that he was a new Christ and
that with him a new revelation began. The Pelagians argued
that human nature benefits by grace at the moment of its creation because it is inconceivable that God should not endow it
generously. Obviously, such good and mature men considered
themselves emancipated from the support that weaker creatures
needed, and thought of themselves as equals with God. Without the stain of original sin an angelic, or indeed divine career
was open because whatever evil existed in the world, could not
be *inside* human nature but only *outside:* in unfortunate circumstances, in sickness and in death. Pelagius actually denied
original sin, arguing that God cannot create souls burdened with
evil.

In our days we hear again that man is good, and that only
exploiting classes, lack of education, nonscientific thinking, etc.,
obstruct this goodness from taking full effect. We are told that
we have reached adulthood since we no longer need God to
explain to us the cause of natural and psychological phenomena.
Of course, Freud and other psychologists deny original sin, and
even when some of them consider guilt *feeling* as therapeuti-
cally salutary, they think of it as something entirely subjective.
Father Teilhard de Chardin who, as priest, could not negate the
doctrine of original sin openly, nevertheless manages to make of
it something impersonal and also automatically reabsorbed in
cosmic progress. He teaches that what we take for original sin is
nothing but groping attempts of evolution to spiritualize the

original matrix, that is matter. These dead-end streets of not quite successful spiritualization, he says, were taken by earlier, insufficiently enlightened theologians, as original sin, that is, sin rooted in nature; but evolution tries new approaches until spirit emerges victoriously and "sin," the last remnants of matter, disappears.[2]

Nothing stands thereafter in the way of mankind to pull itself up by its own forces to inconceivable heights. This process may have been slow and tentative at the beginning of history or of evolution (depending on which science the heretic takes as his basis), but it accelerates when the highway of the future is found. The Manicheists believed that the Perfect, once liberated from evil, become children of light with divine prerogatives. Wycliffe taught a rather pure variety of pantheism according to which everything is God and the real Church is the society of the predestined ones. These same elects appear in the modern heretic's eyes as the scientists, because they are credited to be the only ones understanding the laws of change and the direction in which mankind is moving. Hence we must entrust our destinies to these modern elects who are, in turn, entitled to coerce those among us who would resist their recommendations.

Clearly, we are very far in these considerations from God and Christ. The Pelagians went to the logical end of their arguments and declared that since we are born good and generous, Christ and his Redemption are useless notions. We saw that for similar reasons other heresies arrived at the same conclusion. Some, however, Montanus and others, believed that they are new Christs or at least reincarnations of the original. Indeed, they reasoned, if God sent his Son to bring salvation to a mankind in danger of perdition, He would send Him again among men each time when similar threats appeared. And, as I said earlier, similar threats always existed in the eyes of heretics: evil in the world, immorality of the clergy, abuses in the Church, the pride of the mighty, and so on.

2 "In a world of ascending evolution, sin is often nothing but the refusal to grow in the direction which conscience reveals." *Dutch Catechism* (New York, Herder & Herder, 1967), p. 264.

The tendency today is to believe that mankind, again threatened by evil (by the nuclear bomb, by those who oppose progress, etc.), will this time become collectively mature and good. Our ideologies are messianic, promising salvation just around the corner: the classless society, world government, universal equality, scientifically planned happiness. Under these conditions Christ is either a needless hypothesis or, as Teilhard de Chardin teaches, a symbol of mankind's perfection, emerging at the end of evolution. He will then coincide, physically as well as morally, with the cosmos. Another version of heretical pantheism.

Thus heretics generally conclude that the Church is a concentration of evil (or of imperfectly enlightened) forces, and that true goodness will only be found in the World, the emerging spiritual community of sinless, mature men, possessors of knowledge (gnosis). Wycliffe believed that the Roman church is the synagogue of Satan and the religious orders are diabolical institutions. His intellectual descendants in the twentieth century hold that the Church is an obscurantist institution, its dogmatic edifice a collection of superstitions, its life in a state of arrested growth either since Constantine or since the Council of Trent.

Over against the Church, the World, the secular city is open and full of promise because the motor force of its mechanism is not a collection of archaic models and authoritarian statements but progress and the love of adventure in freedom. When the "new breed" priests exalt the goodness of the World and urge the Church to "join it," they sincerely believe, like the medieval Pure Ones or Calvin's predestined, that a new, more universal, even cosmic Church is bring born, and that they, the new breed priests, with truer insights than the Pope, help its gestation.

The above is not an imaginary list but an all-too-brief summary of views held in the two thousand years of the Church's history. It is an extraordinary proof of divine protection active inside the Church that she could victoriously resist yielding to any one of these theses or to their combination, and remain at the exact point of intersection of the divine and the human.

This is, however, a most difficult equilibrium to maintain, and we may speak of a permanent crisis in the Church when we become aware of the forces trying at all times to disrupt and upset it.

Of what does this equilibrium consist? First, of the admirable insistence that Christ is God and that He gave His guarantee of supreme concern for man. Secondly, of the insistence that God can be known by both faith and reason, although by both only to a limited extent. It follows that faith and reason do not contradict each other, they converge toward the same object. Thirdly, God not being inaccessibly distant (although supernatural and transcendant), His foundation, the Church, carries the divine stamp which confers on her authority over individual souls. The Church is, hence, not merely a human institution responsible solely for our social wellbeing, but a messenger of the divine, and in this capacity she is concerned with our wellbeing, spiritual, moral, and material, in this order. (Evidently, since with our self-interest as guide, we are able to look out for our material prosperity, and need warning only when this search conflicts with our moral and spiritual welfare.)

Fourthly, since God created the world, it is essentially good and permeated with love expressed through the aspiration of all created things toward being. Man is thus not reduced to his own devices in building society, he has the divine injunction and help for it. Nor can this society be purely secular because any attempt to construct such a society, as the story of the Tower of Babel shows, is doomed to failure. Man's need for the absolute cannot find an earthly satisfaction, for this need is rooted in the eternal. Hence an earthly absolute by definition violates this need, for it immediately claims that part which we hold most dear, our spiritual openness and its practical equivalent, personal freedom.

Although having divine protection and approval, society can never become this absolute (that is, perfect) since its architects are sinful, imperfect human beings. Yet, precisely because it can never be a perfect community, *because* it will forever remain "an adversary of the saints" (Maritain), we must relent-

lessly try to improve it. Otherwise it would fall back with a ver-
tiginous speed into inertia and evil. It would be stupid optimism
to expect that this effort of ours can do more than try to keep
such a collapse at arm's length but always menacing, like tropical vegetation always threatens to reconquer human settlements
for the jungle. This situation will not decisively improve until
the end of time, that is, not in the course of history. It is, then,
equally unthinking to expect mankind "to create God" at the
terminal point; without God sustaining us all the time we could
not even reach that terminus, let alone reach it as quasi-divine
beings, ruling creation.

If we understand the two perspectives, one finding expression in heresies, the other in a balanced view of the Church's
teaching, we possess a guideline for orientation in the presently
raging crisis detailed in the following chapters.

III

THE TEMPTATIONS
OF THE
SECULAR CITY

Every organism must show signs of vitality which means that it grows and changes, it can be meaningfully judged and reconsidered. The Church is no exception, but being the repository of Christ's truth, its standard of change is not quite like that of other institutions. Father Yves Congar, one of the theologians perhaps most responsible for initiating the quest for reform which led to Vatican II, wrote this in 1950:

> We are [in the Catholic Church] under the new and definitive dispensation. What belongs by essence to it cannot change and is not subject to any *dépassement:* the repository of apostolic faith, that of the sacraments and of the apostolic powers (priesthood, magisterium, authority), in short, all that constitutes the structure of the Church. This is given, this is final, this can never be reformed.[1]

1 *Vraie et fausse réforme dans l'Eglise* (Paris, Editions du Seuil, 1950), p. 146.

Father Congar then shows that "reform" has meaning only if it remains within the apostolic tradition and is respectful of Church structure and authority. Its chief characteristics are respect, prudence, and patience since it is natural of the Church to live according to the rhythms of life and organic, not revolutionary, development.

There is no doubt that the Church is adaptable to new forms of life and civilization, but also that she does not play a pioneering role in imposing new forms. Which, again, does not mean that the Church is stagnant or backward: in every age it moves in ways specific to its own sense of balance. In her early existence, she saved the best civilizing elements of Rome and transmitted them to Europe's newcomers; as soon as opportunity offered itself, the Church sent out her missionaries to preach the Gospel to non-European populations. And in the age of agnostic, anticlerical and Godless governments, the Church spares no efforts to establish contacts as soon as these regimes mellow sufficiently, so as to keep the link with Catholic citizens under their jurisdiction.

The Church, by the very nature of her message which permeates her missionary zeal, has always been open to the world and has conducted a "dialogue" with it, provided neither openness nor dialogue meant surrender. Yet it would be naïve to close our eyes to the fact that these two terms are parts today of an ideological program. What we have seen in previous chapters tends to convince us that the Church is battered today from inside by neo-Gnostics preaching the separation of the Elect (themselves) from the unregenerate (the institutional Church) until such time that, with the aid of secular doctrines all may be integrated in an earthly Jerusalem.

There is no reason to deny or minimize the need for periodic reforms and adjustments in the Church. A council's task is one of restoring true faith, correcting abuses, rendering doctrinal points more explicit; it is *not* enacting new ideas. Thus it is necessary to examine the "dialogue" and its promoters, and not accept terms only because they have become fashionable.

"Dialogue" means nothing more than conversation, unless it also has a hidden meaning, that of readiness to be persuaded. The way it is used today, dialogue has come to mean the acceptance of the opponent's position in advance of verbal contact with him. The term "dialogue" merely veils this fact with a pretense of equality and equal desire of coming to an understanding. In reality, one of the dialoguers has yielded, and he only insists that certain forms of debate be observed. This has nothing to do with charity; it rather appears as if one partner wished to secure his opponent's triumph in a process of slow surrender. As if legions of Catholics had suddenly discovered that practically everything is wrong with their Church, they cannot make enough genuflections to the world "outside." There is something else at work here than mere philosophical debate and clearly formulated arguments. The painful impression one has is that of a horde of unruly children, thus far checked by discipline, suddenly released at the door of a pastry shop; even high prelates grab the cakes and pies, competing to see who can devour more—that is, who can make sillier and more sensational declarations, who can indulge in more frivolous and scandalous actions.

"My sense of the comic is tickled," writes Jacques Maritain in a book which may well be his testament, "when I witness the rush of persons consecrated to God's service, seeking indoctrination in Freudism. They do it with the most pious, and least scientific, enthusiasm." [2] Indeed, one does not know whether to find it tragic or grotesque when priests and nuns, intellectuals and cardinals beat a masochistic *mea culpa* before the manifestations of frivolousness and passing moods—all in the name of a grimly pursued "modernity." Because, after all, there is nothing more ephemeral than "modernity"; even something shorter than a full lifetime is enough to witness a fair number of "modern," latest truths, each with the claim to being exclusive and final.

[2] *Le Paysan de la Garonne* (Paris, Desclée de Brouwer, 1966), p. 225.

But these are still only superficial attitudes, certainly not to be minimized since they spread scandal and confusion. Behind these attitudes, however, one discovers a far more pernicious situation, the effects of which strike at the foundation stone of the Church. The Church is, of course, permanently exposed to attacks of a doctrinal nature; but since doctrine and behavior are always in subtle harmony, breakdown of behavior, that is, denial of obedience, may have its own sinister consequences. Its origin at the present time is the same as the breakdown of authority in the world at large. There is a switch in the direction of novelty, sometimes called "experimentation," so that the innovators or experimenters acquire prestige for merely doing the unusual. The press, radio, and television can make instant success of a priest as well as of a layman, and this limelight acts then as counterwailing power to hierarchical superiors, up to and including the Pope. In other words, the world offers a refuge to the unruly priest (or the layman) similar to the asylum offered in the past by kings and emperors. The press can take up his defense, foundations may grant him funds to pursue his experiment, professors and panelists are found who discuss the implication. A protective layer is formed around the rebel which, incidentally, blurs the real issue and serves the indefinite maintenance of confusion.

This process facilitates the emergence of a type rather new in the Church, the *Church-intellectual*. For many decades, indeed centuries, this type of man was integrated into the Church's life. It is the de-Christianized milieu and its new feudalisms which brought about his detachment from the Church's body. This does not mean that he ceased being a Christian; but he is also the product of the revolution in the news-carrying and -interpreting media. Hundreds of publications, run by Catholics *qua* Catholics compete, prelates are interviewed like politicians, the latest theological gossip is lapped up by eager readers. The temptation for weak-kneed priests is tremendous to get into the news, to compensate in terms of public attention for a life supposedly retired and modest.

To say something sensational, if necessary even of sacred doctrine, is the newly-acquired lamentable habit of those whom I call Church-intellectuals. Of priests and of laymen speaking as Catholics one expects declarations of a prophetic and spiritual nature. Even when addressing themselves to administrative, educational, or organizational issues, the priestly office imposes on Churchmen the requirement of showing deeper insights and a farreaching perspective. In their talk the transcendental and the mystical is always expected to be at hand. Today something else is added to this expectation: the Church-intellectual is put in a position where it is tempting for him to combine the religious zeal with the here-and-now guidelines that the world wants to be given, or at least wants to discuss. The result is that the Church-intellectual secularizes the Gospel's teaching and makes of it a this-worldly speculative system. Meanwhile the priest who preaches Christ's Gospel and remains a silently efficacious instrument of truth is forgotten, neglected, even a bit despised. He has no news value since he will not answer in a manner contrary to doctrine and tradition sensational polls about priestly celibacy, suppressed sex drives, or the benefits of self-service communion.

The mechanism of our civilization favors the rebellious intellectual, hence the rebellious Church-intellectual too, with his startling theories. What is novel about him in the eyes of the world is that he brings the evangelical zeal to unexamined ideas, half-mature emotions, popular slogans. It is hard to distinguish, again because of the manipulative media, between bona fide expressions of such speculative systems, on the one hand, and opportunism, on the other. Oftentimes we may be confronted with a mixture of the two, as in the example given by Maritain. But what characterizes most of these manifestations is the anxious search of conformity with the ways of the world. This endeavor can have only two explanations: the first is that the Church-intellectuals, following the pattern we analyzed in Chapter II, are again switching their allegiance from the Church to the World because they see in the latter the fulfill-

ment of the Promise. The second explanation is that they want
to acquire the ways and weapons of the World the better to
dominate it. Between the two explanations there is hardly any
contradiction, but both contradict Christ's spirit who refused
Satan's temptation to rule the world provided he agreed to fool
its people. The Church-intellectuals more in the spirit of Dostoevsky's Grand Inquisitor who satisfied people's material wants,
cheating them on their rights as spiritual persons, children of
their Father in heaven.

What shape does the "adjustment to the world" take?
Certain Churchmen, among them prominently the Jesuits, must
have made what seemed to them a precise study of where power
is located in today's world. It is a historical fact that from the
days of their inception the Jesuits sought to influence the powerful through schools, the confessional, and the diplomats' study
—not to leave out the boudoirs of beautiful and influential ladies.[3] After the French Revolution kings fell out of power. "We
are all socialists now," exclaimed Napoleon III one day; power
was passing to socialist labor unions and left-wing parties. German Chancellor Bismarck remarked that sooner or later the
Jesuits will become leaders of the social democrats. In 1872, advised, incidentally, by a Catholic Prince, a Cardinal's brother, he
considerably curtailed what he unflatteringly called the Jesuits'
"parasitic expansion."

It is even more intriguing to recall that Auguste Comte, the
French Positivist philosopher who wanted to establish his own
"positivistic (or scientific) church," approached the Jesuits in
view of an alliance. He was convinced that the "Ignatians" as he
called them (Comte despised Jesus, but had an organizer's es-
teem for the saint of Loyola) would easily renounce Catholic
dogma, and elaborate a cult for the adoration of Mankind. He
entrusted one of his disciples, John Metcalf, with the mission of
contacting the Jesuits of the United States and suggesting that
they cooperate as his, Comte's, "auxiliary forces." Metcalf was

[3] Pascal's *Lettres Provinciales* (1656) brilliantly documents the Jesuit
casuists' rejection of the Church's traditional morality and their elaboration
of a situation ethics.

told not to make concessions to the Jesuit fathers, lest their "habitual disposition for power" might reawaken. When the Jesuit order rebuffed his offer, Comte expressed the belief that not too distant events might ripen the seeds that his offer of a dialogue had sown among the Jesuits.

The Jesuits, then, followed in this by the new breed of Catholic intellectuals generally, know and practice the art of adjustment to the milieu which happens to be in or close to power. Several Jesuit fathers uttered the appropriate noises during the Hitler era, predicting its early mellowing, hence its harmlessness and respectability. In January 1932 the Jesuit Friedrich Muckermann (who later became a violent anti-Nazi) declared that the National-Socialist movement has a good inner core and, duly influenced (!) it might inspire a genuine reform movement. The Jesuit Father Notges wrote at the time that episcopal condemnation of Nazism was conditional. "National Socialism," he wrote, "may one day eliminate from its program and activities all the principles and actions which now clash with those of Catholicism."

Now all these hopes may have been reasonable, yet it is noteworthy that after the defeat of Nazism, the Jesuits switched with sophisticated ease to the other camp. They were soon to discover among their own ranks the man who could provide the shortcut to a new prestige so that the Order might make the world forget its reputation of "Jesuitism." This man was Pierre Teilhard de Chardin whose writings many Jesuits now use as a much-desired synthesis of religion and science. Through these writings they and their followers accept now a new and baffling loyalty to (capitalized) Progress, the religion of the twentieth-century mass-man. Thanks to Teilhard de Chardin, they make now of "the theology of progress a necessity, a fact as sacred as three centuries ago they made of the divine right of kings." [4]

In this brief *aperçu* of Jesuit shifts from support to kings to support of rightist or leftist ideologies attention is called not so much to the Jesuit Order with the exclusion of others, as to the

[4] B. Charbonneau, *Teilhard de Chardin, Prophète d'un âge totalitaire* (Paris, Editions Denoël, 1963), p. 90.

temptation of worldliness which always surrounds the spiritual sphere. Jesuit Hubert Becher acknowledged in 1951 that his Order's "adaptability may create the impression of always being in favorable and advantageous situation." [5] These episodes and statements are mentioned here not in order to cast unfavorable light on individuals or groups, but to show that when certain segments of the Church unleash an imposing mechanism of adaptation to the world's questionable standards or to its power structure, that does not mean that the diagnosis of the Church-men in question is correct. Jesuits (and others) wished to come to terms with national socialism when it seemed to be the wave of the future,[6] and in the same way they now seek alliance with communism and left-wing ideas which appear as a victorious ideology. The history of these attempts is full of temporary successes and final failures; there is no reason for us to assume that the future will be different.

But there is more: the priestly vocation is at once a mystery of charity and of power. The Church maintains these two poles in balance by spiritualizing power and channeling charity toward the service of the concrete individual soul. But charity may also turn to entirely worldly ends, and without passing through Christ's purification, become social action. Power, in turn, may rid itself of spiritual brakes, and its energy may then flow into the sheer practice and enjoyment of it. The world appears then as a more legitimate domain for the released energies since it seems more malleable, more receptive than men's spirits. It is not understood, at least not early enough, that it is also a trap, the wrong end, so to speak, for bringing about change in men.

[5] Quoted in *Der Spiegel*, Nr. 44/1965, p. 77.
[6] Father Teilhard de Chardin saw in national socialism, as indeed in all totalitarian movements and regimes, a positive, although misguided force. In a letter from Peking (August 5, 1941) he wrote: "Fundamentally, the only thing I believe in, the only thing I have chosen, is that one must believe in the Future of the Earth which will coincide with a totalization of Humanity. . . . And this is why since September 1939 I have not cared for this war which, from the French point of view, was merely a defense of egoism and the status quo. The constructive idealism, however distorted, was on the other side." From *Letters to Two Friends* (New York, New American Library, 1967), p. 104.

Perhaps we can now form a more adequate idea of the "dialogue." The Church-intellectuals who engage in it are entangled in their own Church-bred habits: they are divided between their spiritual power and the *libido dominandi* which opens before them unsuspected vistas. For a long time they had felt that they lived in a ghetto where talks about Marxism, psychoanalysis, atheism were passed through the sieve of Catholic doctrine. Suddenly the possibility shines on them of becoming intriguing personalities both in the camp of irreligion which finds them wrong but refreshing, and among Catholics in whose eyes they are the avant-garde, who dare leap over the invisible wall. This is true of priests and lay intellectuals alike. This suddenly acquired freedom, coupled with its sheer news value, makes of these men champions of innovation and emancipation, new Luthers and Calvins. Not because of their special talents or of what they can teach the world, but because of the place they automatically occupy in a sensation-hungry society. This society puts them to a tacit test: will they prove strong enough to resist the temptation of secularized charity, or will they succumb and thereby justify the world's triumphant fall into the abyss of self-love?

Many of them have clearly failed this test since their dream is a dangerous synthesis of religion and the modern world, a kind of lay religion (or secular city) where the priest would merge with the secular leader. This dream is not essentially different from that of the Abbé de Lamennais and many other, so-called utopian socialists of the early nineteenth century. These men had shed the crude atheism of their forebears of the Enlightenment, and while they had only hazy ideas of God, they understood the role of sentiments and loyalty based on faith for the sake of social cohesion. Fond of organizing mankind, they were not inimical to the institutional aspects of the Church, that is to a future World Church of their own construction. A kind of Christian message, but stressing the sentimental at the expense of the rational, permeated their teaching, a message nearer to the Stoics' philanthropy than to Christ's supernatural love. These men were in the forefront of several revolutions, for example that of 1848, and were among the early disciples of Marx. Through several of their adherents and side-movements they were also the ancestors of modern Christian socialism whether in Europe or in Latin America.

Emboldened by the situation described above, their spiritual descendants set out on the conquest of the secular city. The "world" appears to them in such seductive colors, it has so completely become the center of their intellectual gravity, that the ideal for these Church-intellectuals is no longer the Church, but the world. Almost, one might say, the anti-Church. Pretending to introduce the Church's message of love into the world for the latter's benefit, in reality they consider this fusion beneficial, even salvific, for the Church. Henceforward the world appears as the greater, more noble, more promising entity, and the Church as sectarian, partial, petty, and divisive. When this state is reached in their thinking, the Church-intellectuals no longer find it implausible to exalt the salvific messages of the world: science, Marxism, Teilhardism, and others that Maritain calls "ideosophies," that is speculative systems of thought detached from reality, and all the more full of the promise of domination.

All these speculative systematizers want to construct what one of them, Mr. Harvey Cox, describes as the secular city. For reasons at first baffling, Cox and others of similar persuasion speak of themselves and are spoken of as "theologians." What is really meant, however, is that they wish to redirect man's spiritual energies into secular direction, hoping thereby, as Rousseau, Saint-Simon, Feuerbach and many others before them, that nothing will be "wasted" in futile meditation about eternal questions. Mankind's entire dynamism will be put to work for new and tremendous improvements. Thus in the center of these systems we find not God but the perfect society reached through phases of social change. Writes Harvey Cox:

We must learn to speak of God in a secular fashion. . . . It will do no good to cling to our religious and metaphysical versions of Christianity in the hope that one day religion or metaphysics will once again be back. They are disappearing forever, and that means we can now let go and im-

merse ourselves in the new world of the secular city. . . .
The starting point for any theology of the Church must be
a theology of social change.[7]

When the Church-intellectuals assert that man has now
reached maturity through science, technology, socialism, and the
like, they say in reality that Caesar's domain has reached the
threshold of perfection and may begin absorbing that of God.
In their eyes the political community is now emancipated from
God's somewhat burdensome and humiliating supervision; contrary to Christ and Augustine, it is now proposed that the
earthly city is morally self-sufficient, and does not expect to be
made livable through the contribution of the individual believer
as such since it is made livable by the collective forces, technical
improvements, and up-to-date ideologies. Thus the thesis of the
secular-city-builders is not that belief in God and worship in His
temples should be brutally abolished, but that the new man will
not need God and temples since he can live out his entire existence with only Caesar to honor and pay tribute to.

The concept of the "new city" is, of course, as old as the
heretical ramifications of Christian faith. No wonder then that
we find the Church-intellectuals in striking harmony with
nineteenth-century social utopians. The latter recognized the
contributions to society of the Christian religion, but doubted
that faith and doctrine can arouse the constructive enthusiasm
of peoples in this industrial-scientific age. Saint-Simon's "new
christianity" was to be put, like Mr. Cox's, in the service of scientific discoveries, efficient distribution of goods, and of a class
of leaders consisting of bankers, industrialists, inventors, and
managers. The people, now satisfied with their wellbeing, will
follow these leaders, as constituting a new priesthood, as powerful and wise as the priestly caste of ancient Egypt. The supreme

[7] An unsigned article in *Herder Correspondence* (December 1967) suggests that the Church's magisterium should not speak of immutable moral
laws but, learning from the best scientific and cultural knowledge available
at a given time, it should point out the "best means of living it now knows."
It is hard to see the difference between this assignment and that of any social agency.

power would be held by the best twenty-one scientists, gathered in Newton's Council. The pope would be, in Saint-Simon's expectation, a kind of pope of universal science.

This is only one example of the myriad sects and groups which, in the first half of the nineteenth century, tried to reform the Christian religion—recognized as the most perfect and universal faith—so as to help make the new, industrial society cohesive and efficient. A hundred years ago the ideologues bent on this task were no less impressed by what was modern *then:* the steam engine, the photograph, telegraphy, productivity in steel and textile mills, the daily discoveries of science, than are today the Church-intellectuals by what is modern *now:* nuclear power, psychotherapeutic methods, jet travel, fiscal means of preventing inflation, Telstar, and space travel. The temptation is accordingly strong to arrest mankind at this stage, the stage which overawes the leaders of opinion, to proclaim it adult, and celebrate its emancipation from under obscure traditional powers. Saint-Simon perceived that even such a "scientific" society will need an authority to hold it together, a priestly caste leaning on a secular mystery. The Church-intellectuals today would call upon an ideology to play this role; they plan to become the metamorphosed priesthood, no longer called such, but preserving the substance of the old authority and power.

As we see, a whole new speculative system (indeed not the substance, only the terms were new) was needed to explain, justify, and perpetuate the emerging industrial-bourgeois-worker society of the nineteenth century. This was supplied by Saint-Simon, Fourrier, Auguste Comte, and others, and the task was later completed by Marx. In our century the Church-intellectuals have assigned a similar task to themselves: laying the speculative foundations for the secular city modeled after the tremendously productive industrial societies with which they are acquainted. It was inevitable that American intellectuals should take the lead in outlining the ideal city since their country is today the industrial model for the rest of the world.

Their speculation runs like this: Platonic-Aristotelian philosophy and the Christian theology it shaped in the Middle Ages are based on the primacy of the contemplative over the practical. This approach was deep in Greek mentality, and is said to be responsible for the brilliant scientific theorizing of their civilization as well as for their conscious rejection of technical realizations.[8] Thus it is because of an unfortunate event of history that the western world, to which Greek speculation was largely transmitted by the Church, remained for many centuries opposed to technological progress. The root of this attitude can be found in Plato with his distinction between material (inferior) and ideal (real) world, which encourages the search for the absolute but discourages man's conquest of nature.

Our technological civilization—the argument continues— can no longer be tied to such a worldview and its philosophical categories. Not only are our wellbeing and search for happiness linked with the scientific worldview, but our universalist, cosmopolitan tendencies can also be promoted only through technology. For while Greek metaphysics is divisive and creates superiors and inferiors, technology can be acquired by all men and is therefore a force of equalization and democracy.

We see that modern speculation of which the Church-intellectuals are also prisoners remains captive of the framework created by modern industrialization. Let us not deal here with the validity of the attempt to tie theology and doctrine to any one particular form of social development. We deny, of course, this validity on the basis that our reason is not determined, like Marxists and proto-Marxists hold, by the structure of the society in which we live. Let us note only that the Church-intellectuals, imitating their other confreres, believe that the new world (Mr. Cox says "the new Church") is based on the realities of the industrial society. Mr. Cox's "social change," on which all theology must rest, may mean then, if the expression has a meaning at all, adaptation to new methods like automation, to the need of keeping the industrially displaced: the jobless, the handicapped, the undereducated, etc., on the public payroll, to the alleged need of integrating wage-earners with managerial

---

[8] According to Henri Marrou, the reason for Greek rejection of technology was not the availability of unlimited manpower (the institution of slavery), but a conscious choice. See *Education in Antiquity* (New York, Sheed & Ward, 1956).

decision-making, to slum clearing and other programs. But none of these programs require the theological label, let alone a new theology. If the confusion is nevertheless made by the Church-intellectuals, it only means that they address an invitation to the Church to shed its "Mediterranean" structure and Greco-Latin heritage, and adopt the metaphysical underpinnings of Nordic-Protestant societies, so successful in organizing modern industry.

The message of the Church-intellectuals and among them the radical advocates of the secular city is that Catholicism, based on permanence and eternal verities, cannot be adapted to the concept of scientific-industrial progress. The Church's theology, being of Greek inspiration, follows the archetypal thinking of Plato and Aristotle's metaphysics in an "age of change." It is conveniently overlooked that Thomism is much closer to the material world and its existential reality than the idealistic philosophy from Descartes to Kant and beyond to Husserl and Heidegger. The Protestant mentality, on the other hand, is trained to consider history as an ever-renewed protest against a past judged by definition rigid. This mentality becomes much more easily an inspiration of the secular city because it is expected in the light of the rapid secularization and fragmentation of Protestant religion that protest, at some point, will take the entire Christian message for its object. In fact we witness this process today.

The inhabitants of the Secular City are the post-Christian, or at least the post-Catholic men. The sudden preoccupation of Church-intellectuals with the "world," their flattery of what they find therein, means their availability for a despiritualized community of men. In other words, their will to power.

Professor Will Herberg remarked that many Christian leaders today have accepted socialism, even communism as the wave of the future so that they cannot see any more the totalitarian character of the various Soviet regimes. With this kind of State, he concludes his article, no Christian serious about his faith can make his peace.[9] There is, of course, plenty of evi-

[9] "Christian Faith and Totalitarian Rule," *Modern Age*, Winter 1966–1967.

dence supporting Herberg's indictment, and I shall show it in Chapter VI. But the real temptation for these Churchmen is not socialism as such, anyway not the Marxist variety alone, since they mistook Hitlerist socialism also for the wave of the future. Rather, they are tempted by the totalitarian principle in general and are willing to deliver their spiritual power into temporal hands provided they have a share in it.

The Church-intellectuals have long felt that they were removed from power, that the new trends and ideologies bypassed them for decades, even centuries. I mentioned earlier that many of them have been obsessed by the alleged shaping of the modern world outside and even against the Church. Their protestations to the contrary, they do not despise the opportunity of possessing power, of being members in good standing of the Establishment. Power, of course, should not be conceived as the constant use of a brutally exercised authority. First of all, power gives a feeling of satisfaction, particularly to those who had to creep inside it through a back door. In the second place, it procures a satisfaction of being admired, invited, published, and in the limelight, things eminently designed to feed intellectual vanity. And lastly, power facilitates the suppression of opposition, the authority to sit at the censoring end of the new inquisition. This is particularly easy today because the communications media can be used to put a blanket over issues and opponents with the same ease as it can create and amplify news.

Yet, it would be a great mistake to think that the new allies of the Church-intellectuals welcome them as Christians, traditional or "new breed." The condition for joining the Secular City is to become a different Church altogether and an unrecognizable Christianity. In fact, a non-Christianity. The world always extracts a tremendous, literally unpayable price for allowing the Church to join. The price is spirituality that Christ refused to the Prince of this world. In exchange, the world offers *power*, that is, the guarantee against the fear of obscurity, and *success*, that is, the feeling of importance and fulfillment. The dialogue with the world is never on equal terms: since it is hardly ever a genuine dialogue, it is a relationship between superior and inferior. The one who wishes to join must first pass the test of acceptability. At the same time he brings advantages too that the other needs: in the case with which we deal here, that of the Church and the world, the former is useful to the latter exactly in proportion as it still has its roots in the supernatural. The world denies the supernatural, but there will always be those who seek it. If these seekers after God can be neutralized, not by an impossible frontal attack and aggressive negation, but by decapitating their institutional sign and safeguard, the Church, the secular city will no longer have clandestine, inside saboteurs. The Church itself will ferret them out and stand guard over them. Not through physical aggression but by discrediting them intellectually and spiritually. This is the only way for the dialogue to achieve success: for it will no longer be necessary, the partners-in-dialogue will have become indistinguishable.

IV

DIALOGUE WITH PROTESTANTS

What can be the meaning of the Catholic–Protestant dialogue? As we live in the age of public relations and of image-makers, we understand, without approving, why the term "dialogue" takes now the place of earlier and more apt expressions when Catholics prayed for the return of Protestants to the Church. But: Can a mere word, already made meaningless by overuse, form a bridge between two positions of, alas, fundamental difference?

Let us note from the beginning that the position of the Catholic Church as expressed at the Vatican Council has not changed. The *Decree on Ecumenism* approaches the delicate subject of reunion with admirable precision and charity. Our separated brothers, the document states, believe in Christ and are therefore our brothers in the Lord. But this fraternity operates in a state of imperfect union, thus making the Catholic plenitude itself incomplete, the Catholics themselves less fervent, and the Church herself less desirable in the eyes of other Christians. It is clearly expressed that not only the separated ones, the "limbs," suffer from being outside the "general means of salvation," but that the "body" suffers too since it is incomplete without them. But it is affirmed with no less charity in the Vatican *Decree* that only the Catholic Church is the channel of salvation, only to this Body of Christ must be reintegrated those who belong, through baptism, to God's people.

This is, however, not the interpretation of the less precise spokesmen for ecumenism. It is now fashionable, particularly in countries where Catholics and Protestants coexist, to write off the Reformation as the result of a tragic misunderstanding. I noted in another chapter that, according to some self-styled ecumenists, the Council of Trent represented the narrow and regrettable victory of an intransigent party over the better-advised but overwhelmed minority of "bridge builders." This would mean that the faults committed four hundred years ago were exclusively those of the Church.[1]

Once the separation was consummated, there was no easy way back to unity. Unity would have been the harder as in a very short time the Reformist movement subdivided itself into innumerable sects, which prompted Bishop Bossuet a century later to speak of the "variations" of Protestant Churches. The question now is whether the passing of four centuries facilitates the process and the will to liquidate the differences? Those who minimize the difficulties do so very often in bad faith. They say that only a few obstacles stand in the way of reassuring the Protestants: papal supremacy and infallibility, the cult of the Virgin and the saints, and the Roman ecclesial structure together with canon law. To be noted here, as all along the dialogue between the Catholic Church and the rest of the world, is that when faults are mentioned and concessions suggested, it is almost always the faults of the Church and concessions by the Church that are meant. Thus, even for a casual observer it must be clear that the "dialogue" is used to weaken and dismantle the Church, considered to be the prototype of obstacle to progress.

Also to be noted is that while the difficulties of the dialogue are minimized, other difficulties are freely emphasized, namely

[1] For a profound study of the Reformist Thesis, see L. Bouyer, *The Spirit and Forms of Protestantism* (New York, Meridian Books, 1964).

between the Church-intellectuals who are fervent dialoguers and other Catholics who refuse to dilute their faith. The Church-intellectuals not only call attention to the impossibility of any dialogue with the latter, but also do their best to isolate and silence those who are a majority inside the Church, but whose voice is played down instead of amplified by the communication structure. Is this not a recognition that in the dialogue it is not two firm positions that are meant to confront one another but that one side simply yields? This the Church-intellectuals are willing to do—with regard to the Protestants.

This is obvious when we watch the seemingly haphazard events collected by anyone observing the crisis in the Church. All innovations hurriedly introduced have to do with the above-mentioned three objections that the Protestants raise against the Church. The Church-intellectuals relentlessly attack the Pope's position as successor of Peter, as hierarchically supreme, and as infallible (when speaking ex cathedra of faith and morals); they never cease discrediting and ridiculing the Marian cult, calling it childish, primitive, belonging to the pre-modern times when women were not yet equals of men in the home and outside;[2] they remove, embarrassed, signs of the cult of saints, supposedly as remnants of the feudal age when hierarchical superiors were begged to intercede with hierarchically still higher; and they make every effort to dismantle, obstruct, and ignore the ecclesial structure, declaring that decrees from Rome are not valid, that they evaluate erroneously the local situations, or are simply not to be carried out.

Any number of instances belonging to these three categories could be mentioned; they fill with scandal the Catholic publications. But let us take the declaration on the dialogue at its face value and inquire about its merits. If this inquiry is to be serious, it must penetrate to the roots of the separation and

---

[2] Let us remember the storm raised by the Liberal Catholic press when, at the end of the third session of Vatican II (December 1964), Pope Paul called for the special act of grace by Mary, Mother of God. According to these press reports, the Pope's words created a "painful impression" among progressive bishops and Protestant guests. Let us also bear in mind Calvin's words: "Whores are more modestly attired than images of the Virgin in the Papists' temples." (*Inst. Christ.* Ch. XI)

must ask whether Catholicism and Protestantism are compatible. This can be done only if Protestant thesis, doctrine and
attitude, are laid bare, from Luther and Calvin to the theologians who shape Protestant thought in this century.

We have seen that most deviations from Catholic teaching
have had a gnostic inspiration. And that the essence of the
gnosis is that God is distant, unknowable by reason, accessible
only through faith. But while reason represents a common platform, faith is different in each of us, and its intensity is incom-
municable. From the beginning the Reformers stressed the primacy of faith and its unique salvific character. Its only external
proof for the individual was to possess the vocation to preach
the Word. "The vocation of the elect," wrote Calvin, "is like a
testimony of their election. . . . On the contrary, the damned
are recognizable by their lack of knowledge of the Word and the
sanctification of the Spirit." [3] And again (in Chapter XXVI):
"the certitude of our vocation makes us sure of our being elect."
Similarly Luther: the real Church is the congregation of Christians professing to be saved only by faith in Christ. The ministry
consists in the preaching of the Word. Protestantism, writes Father Yves Congar, wants nothing more for Christianity than a
prophetic status, consisting of divine acts without any link to
man or ecclesiastic operations.[4] Luther himself disliked using
the term *Kirche* (church) and preferred *Christentum*, the
(noninstitutional) gathering of Christians.

In its clearest form we find this doctrine in Karl Barth's
theology, where God touches the human sphere only peripher-
ally, not authorizing any relationship between the visible
Church and grace and salvation. True, Barth's theology was a
reaction to the sentimental and comfort-seeking liberal Protestantism he found as being popular at the time of his youth; he
therefore represents a rigorous neo-Calvinism in which God is
like an autocrat, intervening in human affairs when he pleases,
yet never giving His Word for permanent human use. Thus all
so-called externals or incarnations of the Word, for example, the

[3] *Institutio*, Bk. III, Ch. XXI.
[4] *Op. cit.*, p. 439.

Church and the sacraments, are human and this-worldly, not binding on God who is *totaliter aliter* ("wholly other").[5] The institutionalized Church is especially not legitimate since it is the creation of men corrupted to the marrow by the original sin. Christ did not come to prop up this corruption through the instrumentality of more worldly bodies, but to replace them with His own Word. Thus it is the Word of Christ which is Church, sacraments, and means of salvation, and the Word is the sign of the election of the elect. It is known through Scripture; all other addition or tradition are mere human inventions.

It follows from this that the real Church, precisely because it has no institutional shackles, is in constant renewal; one state of Protestant confession of faith gives way to another, ad infinitum. The real Church is *semper reformanda*, according to the famous formula. Writes pastor Albert Finet, leading French Protestant: "Protestantism is characterized by a state of permanent reform and search." This is meant to avoid the kind of fixity for which Protestants have always blamed the Roman Church with her elaborate ceremonies, liturgy, hierarchy, and authoritarian structure. The Protestant, on the contrary, with the burden of his conscience fully on him, is supposed never to yield to the temptation of becoming rigid in his faith; hence Protestant councils are to purge themselves periodically of past beliefs and attitudes, and set out resolutely on a new course.

On the other side of Barth, among the liberal Protestants, the Holy Spirit has come to be identified with the voice of individual conscience, and religion with a system of changing symbols. Both schools of thought agree that God is practically irrelevant for human affairs, either because He is infinitely distant, receding from us like the galaxies in Einstein's expanding universe, or because our feeble reason can form only very vague

[5] This is also the position of Pastor Albert Finet. "For the Protestant that I am," he writes, "the Gospels do not represent a confirmation of natural theology or morals, they are the source of morals and theology. The only visible sign of the Church's reality is that God's Word is faithfully preached therein and the sacraments are correctly celebrated." (*Le Monde*, December 23, 1965)

ideas about Him. For Barth, man, uncertain about God's wishes in the secular domain, should take matters, including political ones, in his own hands, making of these matters a kind of a game (since God's eyes are not upon it), yet serious for what is at stake in earthly terms. For Reinhold Niebuhr God is more relative. In a recent interview printed in *Commonweal* about the "God is dead" theologians, he declared:

> I think they are stupid. Stupid because they don't realize that all religious convictions and affirmations are symbolic. . . . They say that it is necessary to clear the ground for new conceptions. What does that mean? Someone is going to rush in with some new symbol. The Communists' have already given us a new symbol that has proved inadequate. Rather than merely clear the ground of all irrelevant myths and conceptions, they should work toward a new and relevant conception of God and His mysteries.

For Barth's and Niebuhr's more liberal confreres, for Tillich or Bonhoeffer, only the earthly involvements, minimized by Barth, are serious, because with science explaining the universe, we no longer need God. Tillich still speaks of the ground of our being, a moral-psychological amalgam of "ultimate concerns" with guilt and death; but his God too is inaccessibly distant, ready, like Bonhoeffer's God, to advise modern man to turn secular. God, the latter wrote, deliberately calls us in this twentieth century to form a Christianity that does not depend on the premise of religion.

Several things are at once apparent from these few remarks. The central Protestant thesis is that for one reason or another man cannot count on God; he must count, rather, on his own efforts, whether this fact fills him with anguish or with optimism. Some thinkers stress anguish, others optimism, but at any rate the source is common. As is common also the thesis that God has not authorized anybody to represent Him among men, has not instituted a Church to bear testimony to His Word. Only individuals may feel capacitated to speak out like prophets, and their guarantee in doing this is not more than a personal sense of vocation. Outside a very narrow religious activity, the Christian's sphere is then indistinguishable from his sphere as a layman, a secular man. And whereas the Church is invisible, the world and even the organization of the ecclesia are, according to Luther himself, within the sphere of action of the Prince, that is, of the secular power. It follows, according to Karl Barth, that the political community is either a company of individuals where evil and abuse are everpresent, or a strict and stultifying organization with the constraint and boredom of barracks life. Why then should the Christian be interested in this silly succession of events? Even a senseless history and an evil State ought to elicit his consent, not positively but because of his basic indifference. "The fact that the State could actually honor evil and punish the good [as in the case of Pontius Pilate] may be quite true, but it cannot alter its mission, hence it does not affect the Christian attitude toward the State." [6]

It is clear from this that the only essential thing for Luther or Barth is the community formed around Christ's Word; all the rest is so contemptible as to be left to Caesar's domain. Caesar's domain in Luther's time was that of the German princes who seized the opportunity offered by the Reformation to confiscate Church property and go beyond the sphere of their own legitimate temporal power by interfering with the spiritual domain, their citizens' conscience. In our time, Caesar's domain is the vast de-religionized, indeed antireligious world of Hitlerism, Marxism, and the various "secular cities." Thus the internal logic of Protestantism of Luther's and Barth's variety exposes it to dissolution and absorption in the outside world which may or may not be hostile to religion, which may indeed be sentimentally religious today, agnostic or militantly atheistic tomorrow.

This whole approach may, however, be entirely reversed, and it still finds justification among Protestant theologians. Barth himself, in obvious contradiction with the above, launched a savage attack against the national-socialist State, insisting that "it is necessary, *now, now, now,* [his italics] to act,

[6] *Community, State, and Church* (Three Essays) (New York, Anchor Books, 1960), p. 131.

help, fight with might and main." And, in *A Letter to American Christians*, he wrote that "the war is a beneficial and merciful thing which is in the truest interest of even those most directly hit thereby." [7]

Thus opposite attitudes may be derived from the initial Protestant inspiration. The early Reformers found proof of degeneracy in the corruption of the Roman Church, but, writes E. L. Tuveson, "the arguments for the decay were to be replaced by an overwhelming confidence that God's method in His universe is one of betterment . . . in nature, society as well as in the Church." [8] Speaking of Burnet, Tuveson adds: "In Burnet, the Augustinian emphasis upon the saving experience of the *individual* is submerged in the concept of the *whole* of mankind being led, step by step, slowly, but surely, back to its original Eden." [9]

We had here the illustration of the Protestant contradiction: on the one hand, no earthly community is recognizable as Church, as guide for the faithful, as transmitter of tradition;[10] on the other hand, there is optimism concerning the world which will become paradisiacal, perfect. This is the line of thinking taken by Burnet himself (1728), by his contemporaries Thomas Sherlock and W. Worthington, and before them, in the middle of the seventeenth century, by John Henry Alsted. It is also the central point in the dominant sector of contemporary German and Anglo-Saxon theology.

In fact, however, the contradiction is apparent only and the unity of the Protestant thought may be easily demonstrated. In the name of Gospel purity Calvin and Luther imposed such a

[7] He reverted to indifference in the face of the postwar communist state. The pretext was that the powerful of the world (he meant the United States and the Vatican) are anti-Communist anyway.

[8] *Millennium and Utopia* (New York, Harper Torchbook, 1964).

[9] *Idem*, p. 155. The rest of the passage is worth quoting: "This idea of progress is to be differentiated from the traditional views of Christian advancement. There is certainly, said Saint Vincent of Lerins, progress in Christ's Church. Yet, he added—and the qualification is of prime importance—on condition that it be real progress, not alteration of the faith."

[10] Calvin in his Preface to the *Institutions*: "They [the Catholics] are far from truth when they only recognize a visible Church . . . . This is the core of our controversy."

narrow framework on their followers that the energy inherent in the will to be saved, combined with structural variations, compelled later Protestant generations to broaden indefinitely the field of application. If, indeed, the Gospel alone is the guide, then the mere uncertainty of the preacher's vocation (*la pure predication de la Parole de Dieu*—Calvin) authorizes, even obliges, its never-ending interpretation. Catholics have no such problem because tradition, today so maligned, is the naturally and organically growing explanation of Gospel teaching to successive generations and circumstances. Those who, inside the Church, speak today of updating, do it out of ignorance or ill will; the updating has been a continuous process in the Church since the very beginning, and its history is called tradition, itself not stagnant but growing by accumulation as well as rejection.

Such a process is forbidden to the Protestant who must either choose among those who seem pure as preachers, or go it alone and trust his own interpretation of the Word. In both cases the burden finally rests on his own shoulders.[11] In centuries used to theological arguments this still created lively interest and controversy. Today, however, in the "age of unbelief," the reaction among many Protestants to the Protestant choice is either religious indifference or the transformation of the invitation to "trust individual conscience" into "trust individual reason." This is what happened to liberal Protestantism which then followed reason in all of the latter's peregrinations in the jungle of modern philosophy where reason became ideology, psyche, collective conscience, world opinion, and what have you.

What could be reason's field of application according to the Protestant position? Calvin insisted (*Inst.*, Bk. II, Ch. V.) that our mind is so completely alienated from God's justice that we can only "conceive, imagine and understand evil, iniquity, and corruption." [12] In desperation, this mind turns then toward

11 As Luther wrote in his tract on *The Freedom of a Christian* (1520), "Since faith alone suffices for salvation, I need nothing except faith exercising the power and domination of its own liberty. This is the inestimable power and liberty of Christians."

12 This singularly restricts, if indeed, accepts as valid, the domain of human reason and philosophy. The summa of what God wanted to teach to

exclusively mundane matters, although it may bring to them all the untapped religious zeal. And since the organization and affairs of the political community were declared purely mundane matters by the Reformers (as also by Barth), the building of a purely *secular* society becomes a quasi-*religious* obligation for the Protestant. Hence the obvious heretical overtones of the "secular city" debate: nobody, no true Catholic anyway, questions the validity, necessity, even essential goodness of secular society, that is the political expression of the temporal order. Together with an organized strong Church to call men to their spiritual duties, an organized strong temporal society makes up the diptych of life as Christ and Saint Paul, as well as the popes, always and consistently taught. The worm is introduced in the apple by the Protestant thesis with the assertion that all power belongs to the secular province, that the religious community should remain aloof to this domain and, in fact, should accept even a harsh authority as a deserved punishment for our sinfulness. The preachers of the secular city, Protestant and Catholic, say now in essence that we should follow their particular illumination, the word for which their subjective sense of vocation is the only guarantee. Their light tells them that God wants the secular city even at the price of His own elimination; that God calls us to godlessness through the mouth of these new prophets.

This is, indeed, the only thing remaining for God to do if we listen to some Protestant preachers. For the undermining of the last ground of Protestantism, Scripture, has been going on for some time so that the individual Protestant has been left nothing to stand on. I am referring to Rudolf Bultmann's efforts

---

us are His words, Calvin claimed; when Luther was asked if it is possible to know God with natural means (arguments drawn from nature as well as from man's natural lights) he answered in the negative. Thus, for Luther and Calvin there can be only theology, no valid philosophy. See Étienne Gilson, "Christianisme et Philosophie," *Itinéraires,* May 1967. The chapters referred to here, the critique of Protestantism, are based on Gilson's lecture before the students of the Protestant Theological Faculty, Paris, 1936. The whole work, under the above title, was first published by Librairie philosophique J. Vrin, Paris, 1936.

to "de-mythologize" the Gospels, the life of Christ, and early Church history. But before speaking of Bultmannism, we should point out again that this enterprise of robbing even the Gospel of its validity—hence the Protestant Christian of the last trusted source of his faith—is not in contradiction with the Protestant inspiration. If nothing, absolutely nothing, remains of traditional Christianity, the Protestant may take the last leap and appoint a god within his own conscience. He will then mistake the very enthusiasm with which he regards himself as carrier of God for genuine religious feeling, indeed for the only true and pure and irrefutable religion. He will then claim that his actions are dictated by this inner god with whom he by definition communicates daily. The only difference between this attitude and that of the Reformers four hundred years ago is that they trusted God to reveal Himself to each of us personally, whereas today we trust ourselves with having a truly divine conscience. God has been absorbed by the soul, the Protestant tension has been resolved. Each of us is his own trusted preacher.

All that Bultmann did was to render this last temptation of the Protestant mind explicit and to lend it scholarly support, at least the semblance of it. In his view, as in Barth's, God is "radically other," He is the "absolute beyond," totally inaccessible. Barth's conclusion is that therefore the world is not organized by God, and that no Church can claim to be founded by Him. This position, however, still leaves the Gospels intact, insofar as they transmit Christ's teaching. Bultmann goes further. The first community of Christ's disciples, he says, expected the parousia, the immediate return of Christ in glory. As this did not happen, generations of Christians began settling down and the Church came into existence. Obliged to justify this existence beyond the obvious meaning and scope of Christ's teaching,[13] the Church elaborated the New Testament and put together a plausible narrative for posterity. Evidently, this narrative is pure

[13] In his Gifford Lectures (1955) in Edinburgh, Bultmann said: "It is true that Jesus preached to gatherings of people, but in such a way that only individuals were called to follow him."

myth, a myth which translates otherworldly preoccupations into the terms of this world (*der Mythos objektiviert das Jenseits zum Diesseits*).

The Christian, Bultmann writes, is not authorized to speak of God in the light of human reason because he would then make of God an object of human discourse, a worldly matter manipulable by man. Therefore there is no theology or doctrine which would contain verities revealed by God; God has never revealed anything. Still, salvation is possible but it is derived from faith, an *unmotivated* act by which we "consider" the cross on which Jesus died as the Cross of Christ.[14]

This leaves everybody free to decide for himself whether there is a God, whether faith makes sense, and whether salvation is worthwhile. Again, everything depends on the decisions of the "internalized god," in other terms subjective conscience. Bultmann, however, gave indirect indications that even this internalized god is a kind of mythological remnant and that our conscience will have to be freed of impregnation by gnostic mentality. He quotes Hans Jonas approvingly about the gnostic view: "After the decay of the mythological view of the world, the world will now be left in its pure, indifferent objectivity, thus offering free scope for a purely secular scientific observation, whereas for the ancient world theology and physics had never been divorced from one another."[15]

Those who think that when Bishop John A. Robinson equates God with love, and love with social work, he becomes a rather marginal popularizer of other Protestant thinkers, themselves too radical to be representative, must realize that in his primitive way the Bishop conveys faithfully the convergent views of the theologians of the main current of Protestantism.

---

[14] Bultmann makes a typically Hegelian distinction between historical events (for example, the Crucifixion) and events pertaining to the supposed essence of history (the consideration of the Crucifixion as a salvific act). But it is our subjective decision which is which, and in this case the Crucifixion cannot be regarded as a historic drama of universal validity. It would be more honest, remarks Ugo Lattanzi, to speak of a subjective phenomenon only. See "Les Synoptiques et l'Eglise selon Bultmann," *Itinéraires*, January 1967.

[15] *Primitive Christianity* (New York, Meridian Books, 1956), p. 167.

But we may still legitimately wonder why Catholics would recommend "dialogue" with *these* Protestants, instead of offering them the light by which to leave their darkness.

The justification of the dialogue cannot be, therefore, the desire to work out some doctrinal compromise. What remains is the unreasonable hope entertained by some Catholics that through the assimilation of the Protestant worldview the process of civilizations founded on this worldview might be imitated. The features envied are *indifference* to divine and theological concerns mistakenly labeled *tolerance*; a this-worldly orientation; the zeal to establish favorable conditions in a scientifically organized society. In this way the many inequalities and conflicts plaguing Catholic societies may be eliminated or lessened.

I became most aware of this motivation in certain Catholic circles while traveling in Latin America. These circles are now promoting on that continent a quasi-revolutionary *cambio de estructuras* in the name of the following reasoning: Europe, at least Catholic Europe, was not prepared for the Industrial Revolution when it came. The Church allowed social antagonisms to grow and tear apart the fabric of society. Industrialization and modernization are now imminent in the Latin-American countries. The Church must not only be prepared, but also should be in the forefront of proposing the reforms which will render societies more flexible and will cushion the shock.

This is not the place to examine whether these assumptions are correct or incorrect in the concrete situation of the Latin-American continent. But it is interesting to note that the so-called "progressive" Catholics attribute the reform-mindedness to the Protestant milieu, although they believe that the Catholic Church would be better inspired in doing the job: it would not allow an essentially Protestant-type capitalism to conquer the Latin-American mentalities and markets. At any rate, these circles consider modern efficiency in production, distribution, and services a byproduct of certain Protestant traits. In order to obtain the same results, these Catholics reach the conclusion that they would have to streamline their religion.

Another reason for the rapprochement with Protestants is

that the Church sincerely wants to avoid even the threat of a new Reformation. The Church cannot sustain a new schism, a new separation in a world of multiplying and clashing ideologies. One way of preventing it is to neutralize in advance those who are alert to the danger created by the dialoguing Church intellectuals and would mount, already at this point, the "counter-Reformation." It is, naturally an unresolvable question whether the decline in Church authority and doctrinal unity has or has not reached the danger point. It is similarly debated whether the Church lives at present through a crisis bigger or smaller than it experienced after 1517 when Luther challenged it openly. The interval of four and a half centuries may have rendered the two situations incommensurable. But the inclination, and even perhaps the decision in some circles seem to be that (1) the Church may survive only in unity, or at least in symbiosis with Protestantism, and that (2) Christianity itself may only have a future by uniting its dispersed forces and collectively adjusting to the modern world, itself of Protestant inspiration and preferences.

Two questions must be asked at this point. Was the Church poorly advised when she launched the Counter-Reformation at the Council of Trent? Is it better advised today when it wants to engage in dialogue with Protestantism it repudiated four hundred years ago?

Both questions have been answered on the doctrinal level. The Church in the sixteenth century, after sixteen hundred years' experience with heresies, understood clearly the danger that threatened from the Reformers' side, and acted both in the interest of the purity of the faith and of institutional self-defense. Since then historical events have made Protestantism less of a danger, but that was due not to any change in the Protestant principle but to the slackening of Protestant zeal (and to shattered unity), on the one hand, and to Catholic fidelity to Trent, on the other. It is argued now that an era has come to an end, that in today's tolerant world (sic!) the Church may lower its defenses, otherwise it will remain alone with its intransigent stance.[16] This is, of course, nonsense: according to Christ's warning the Church may never let down its defenses because its enemies are, and will always be, legion. And while more determined immediate enemies can now be identified (the Marxists, for example) than Protestantism, the Protestant thesis, with its always open temptation of dissolving itself in the secular city, remains the more permanent adversary.

In a powerful or diluted form, its basic subjectivism feeds the opposition to the Church, particularly today when, mostly under Protestant influence, reason finds itself in a discredited role and yields to emotionalism. A remedy to this state of affairs would come if we recognized that the Reformation was not a historical accident but that men who thought very differently about ultimate questions drew the legitimate conclusion of not being able to remain under the same roof. Thus only such a chief exponent of ecumenism as Hans Küng can assert that "our schism [with the Protestants] goes back not simply to the weakness and evil concupiscence in human nature, but to a particular historical event independent of any individual living today." [17] On the contrary: this historical event was merely a particular explosion at a certain time of deep philosophical differences ripening at least since William Occam. True, none of the protagonists live today, we were hardly in need of being told *that*; but the spiritual descendants are among us, and part of this chapter is devoted to the explanation why nothing essential changed this spiritual family since the sixteenth century.[18]

If Hans Küng insists so strongly on Reformation as an historical accident, the reason is that he wants to draw a parallel between the sixteenth century and today. He holds that with a

[16] "Absolutist methods which have disappeared in the civil sphere along with absolutist rulers, to some extent prolong their anachronistic existence within the Catholic Church." (Hans Küng, *Freedom Today* [New York, Sheed and Ward, 1966], p. 58.)

[17] *The Council, Reform and Reunion*, p. 95. Sheed and Ward, New York, 1961.

[18] According to L. Bouyer, on most issues Karl Barth is more intransigently Calvinist than was Calvin himself.

little good will the Church could have avoided driving her "re-
newalists" into Calvin's arms so that they had to become heretics; with similar good will the Church can prevent another
schism today. What is the definition of "good will" in this matter? In Küng's obvious interpretation, purely and simply yielding
to pressure—in the present case to the pressure of introducing
reforms he approves, reforms which, unless they affect the faith,
should be welcomed, he says, with open arms. Note that Küng
spoke of good Catholics who became heretics when driven by
the Church's firmness into Calvin's Geneva. But suppose they
were heretics *before* their migration, and that the Church drove
them out for that very reason. Why does a Catholic become
heretic? Is it because the Church is intolerant? Does then the
Church create heretics merely by having a set of doctrines and
beliefs? Should it *not* have a set of doctrines and beliefs? Should
it modify them in each case to suit the objectors?

In a sense this is what Küng desires. Like all Church-
intellectuals, he remains in fervent admiration before a particular form of present civilization, and, from love for his Church
that we must suppose sincere, he would like to adapt this
Church to this civilization. He is quite embarrassed, for example, that Catholic "superstitions, medieval in form, remain forever a byword among Protestants." [19] He mentions pictures,
statues, devotional objects, novenas, indulgences, apparitions,
pilgrimages. Now, let us ask, why should we be embarrassed by
these manifestations of Catholic piety? Do Protestants really
scorn Catholics on this account? The matter is worth investigat-
ing.

Paul Tillich saw the decline of Protestantism in the fact
that the bourgeois class, with belief only in rationality and progress, expropriated the religious sphere and desiccated it. With
the help of this class, Protestantism destroyed what it despised
in Catholicism, the magic element. Tillich says he became a religious socialist because he had understood what a powerful inspiration magic is for men, and because, in his view, socialism was
to restore it to our civilization. Better said, socialism together

[19] *Idem*, p. 123.

with religion, because socialism alone, with its extreme materialism, helps only maintain the spirit of capitalism. Religion adds to it the sacraments, the fulness of the faith, and the supernatural.

Tillich's socialist bias is not our concern here. But we may detect what he tried to reactivate for Protestantism. Anybody who has seen the crowds of worshipers in front and inside the basilica devoted to the Virgin of Guadelupe in Mexico City understands what Tillich meant with his nostalgic call for the "magic" in religious life and what should be rather called existential attachment to the life of faith. The faithful approach the church from the far end of the immense plaza on their knees, and it is on their knees that they cover the distance to the entrance. Inside the church Catholic life is nothing if not vibrant: myriads of ornaments catch the eye, the little people mix with rich ladies, children cry, the sick are brought in to make their devotions; all bring their concerns, illnesses, gratitudes, and hopes. One great prayer and adoration ascends to Heaven, illuminated by hundreds of candles with their flames reverberating on silver, gold, and precious stones.

Now let us switch to Mass in Africa, to Indian processions on the Guatemalan high plateau or in Vietnamese parishes, things I have had the great good fortune of witnessing. Imagination is captivated by the Church's inexhaustible past and inventiveness, indefinitely adaptable to local taste and ancestral custom, yet stamped with universal Christian symbols. The flags, statues, beads, the gold of Taxco's baroque church and of Bahia's San Francisco, the piety of black priests and nuns in the Congo or Senegal, are not objects of scorn but signs of the Church's universality and universal ability to speak to the mind, the emotions, and the senses.

When Küng criticizes it, and worse: is embarrassed by it, this is a sign of his uncritical admiration of precisely those dry aspects of Protestantism that Paul Tillich deplored as destructive of the faith. This admiration stems from a mistaken concept of efficiency, and, of course, from a misjudgment of what constitutes the avant-garde. I have always found it pitiful

and grotesque when magazines published by priests or priest de-
baters on radio show themselves exaggeratedly emancipated,
when they choose films, plays, and books to review and issues to
discuss which deal with gross and vulgar aspects of sex. These
poor priests try to live down their sacerdotal status instead of
living up to it, embarrassing and angering in the process their
listeners, particularly the young whom they so desperately hope
to please. But while this is merely painful because ludicrous,
Hans Küng's attitude, shared with others, leads to scandals and
tragedies in the life of individuals and church communities. Innumerable examples could be listed of the brutality and ignorance with which priests, in their iconoclastic zeal, destroy and
discredit venerable habits and objects. This is perhaps the most
immediate damage done by the dialogue, a damage Luther came
to deplore in his time.[20]

Protestantism has weakened not only tradition, but also the
esthetic, existential side of man. This is what Paul Tillich deplored in the passage above. It was a unique impoverishment of
the religious domain when all over the northern half of Europe
churches, statues, missals, woodcarvings were whitewashed,
broken, crushed, and burned, but the spirit in whose name it
was done was more devastating still. Protestantism generally denied the rights of the body and of the senses, and its puritanic
variety inflicted horrible punishments on the most innocent expressions of earthly joy. It is no exaggeration to say that the
Reformation dealt a serious blow to the Renaissance nurtured
by the Orthodox and Catholic Churches, because the Reformers
held that inner light, the sole contact of man with God, is pros-
tituted by external support. Any kind of visible sign of this radical internalization was, in Luther's judgment, the enthronement
of the things of (a corrupt) nature, and more: the affirmation of
their sufficiency in lieu of the invisible Church.

When Chateaubriand wrote his new-style apologetics, *Le
Génie du Christianisme*, he was able to prove without possibility of contradiction that art in the West was intimately linked

[20] Two Councils, the second Nicea (787) and the fourth Constantinople
(868) condemned iconoclasm.

with the life of the Church and that it actually owed its existence to the inspiration of Christianity and the Church's generosity. Through repeated "renaissances": under Charlemagne and the Irish monasteries, in the twelfth century and in the fifteenth, then the Baroque, architecture, music, poetry and the theater, painting, sculpture, and the minor arts, all were celebrating Christ, the Virgin, the saints, and the truths and the values of Christendom. They were not an addition to or an outgrowth of faith, they were parts of it like artistic expression has been part of man since the earliest ascertainable traces from Neolithic statuettes to the cave paintings of Lascaux and Altamira.

It is the great drama of the West since the Reformation that Protestantism, while demythologizing religion, also stripped it of its human richness, the kind of richness that gives visible and tactile support to spiritual life, to prayers and to mystical experience. It is characteristic that while Protestantism gave rise during these centuries to the modern forms of social and economic concern, it deemphasized the existential and the mystical. It gave birth to only one religious genius, Sören Kierkegaard, who ended up in despair, absurdity, and irrationality. He could not find in his religion channels for his genius.[21]

Yet, we are now invited to perpetrate a Protestant-style iconoclasm. The reasons given vary, but the basic motivation is the same: a supposed purification of the Church and the transformation of the church buildings into assembly rooms where one may have no solace, only sociological and psychological "experiments." One reason given is that the Church has shown too long an attitude of "triumphalism" which coincided with its alleged political power and superiority stance. The "new" Church must show modesty as only one among the many faiths (ideologies) by which mankind lives. The other reason is that in order to reconquer the working classes, pomp and circumstance must be eliminated and the workers approached on Sunday in an en-

[21] Three critics, the Danes Georg Brandes and Harald Höffding, and the French Paul Petit observe that in his later years, Kierkegaard was getting nearer a Catholic orientation.

vironment similar to the one where they spend their time the rest of the week. This is, of course, a false reasoning, and first of all contemptuous of workers. Everybody likes to dress up for solemn occasions, particularly when such occasions are rare. Why not then dress up the environment too, why not greet with beauty and ceremony the God who visits us? But, of course, the Church-intellectuals have a falsely romantic idea of the "worker," formed in the time of Lamennais when it was unbelievable that the working class might cease to suffer from economic inequities and might want to become indistinguishable from other people, Wednesdays as well as Sundays. Yet, a M. Roland Ruelle, not afraid of ridicule, dared write the following: "A worker does not pray with the same words as an ambassador! Why don't we admit varieties of liturgy according to whether we are in a student parish or a worker parish? Priests ought to have the freedom to adopt their Mass to the environment." [22]

Not only M. Ruelle, but also a theologian with the reputation of K. Rahner, S.J., suggests similar breaking-up of liturgical unity, in this case for the young who seek a feeling of security in "the gang," and who "cannot as yet take possession of the whole of Christianity." [23] But this much could be said of any and all of us. Why then this separation of youth, of workers, of students, of ambassadors, why this breaking-up of liturgical and other unity when, on the other hand, the Church-intellectuals desire unity with Protestants and with members of other faiths? To speak of the young people only whom Rahner wishes to protect from the full truth of Christianity, are they not asked today to join the labor market, to wear the uniform, to become members of the Peace Corps? Are they not hailed as more mature than similar generations in the past? Why then consider them less able to grasp Christianity's relevance? Why play special music for them (and no doubt also for workers, students, and ambas-

[22] *Temoignage Chrétien,* November 21, 1963.
[23] *The Christian Commitment* (New York, Sheed and Ward, 1963), p. 158.

sadors), why spoil their taste with jazz Mass when, on the other hand, the Church-intellectuals insist on making culture accessible to all classes of people? In other words, why not play Bach instead of rock 'n' roll to workers and students, as well as to ambassadors?

Statements like Rahner's serve as a prelude and justification for the iconoclastic excesses in French churches where, in the name of updating, misled and browbeaten priests are vandalizing their own churches, destroying or selling the art of centuries. Not, mind you, the stilted and sugar-coated Sulpician products of the last century which would bring no appreciable price and no damage to the Church's patrimony, but medieval retables, tabernacles, statues of saints, baroque candelabra, and the like. One tabernacle was widely shown in French picture magazines as serving now as a doghouse in the new owner's garden! Art lovers and critics, among them men and women known for their religious disbelief, and even the State, call the clergy to order, to the respect if not of their religion, at least of its artistic expression, the national treasure of France.

In this frenzy of destroying what is venerable and beautiful a special mentality is at work which does not stop at the transformation of a beautiful church into an "industrial decor" for the workers, but dictates, with the barbarian's logic, acts of personal brutality too.[24] Dale Francis reported a few years ago in *The Critic* some of these acts of updating which shock and baffle American Catholics. Outstanding was the example of a young priest who, upon seeing the rosary in an older priest's hand, grabbed it and shoved it into the wastebasket. Similar are the words of a French priest to a lady asking him to say Mass for a defunct member of her family. "How is it possible that you still believe in such things?"

A dialogue, even when one partner is convinced in advance that his opponent is right, needs two partners. It can be asked

[24] Cf. the articles by the art critic André Chastel, "Mort aux retables," in *Le Monde*, February 17, 1965.

how Protestants respond to the suddenly extended hands, in what manner do they judge the quasi-Reformation conducted inside and by the Church.

There are of course not one but many reactions. Generally they are characterized by surprise to see the Church, particularly its so-called progressive elements, accept words and acts it has rejected for four centuries, and before it, for sixteen centuries. Hopes are expressed that Rome will not stop halfway but give up its untenable positions one by one. Surprise and hope are, however, accompanied by a measure of skepticism and a shade of contempt. Under the surface of friendly, almost welcoming words, the Protestant leaders hardly hide their little regard for this delayed surrender, but they also ask themselves whether it is motivated by a sincere change of heart or by a Machiavellian design to confuse so-far settled issues. "The Council was a step in the right direction," these people say, "but it did not go far enough. It merely tried to save the central error by making some spectacular but largely meaningless concessions." One can also feel behind many Protestant statements the tacit concern that if the Catholic Church becomes, instead of a rock, a marshy field, the very meaning of Protestantism will have suffered at the core, namely the *act of protest*.

One thing, however, is crystal clear: Protestant spokesmen have no intention of giving up any part of their doctrine or of making concessions of any sort. Once again, the dialogue means that the Catholic Church, *only* the Catholic Church, should change, as an old stubborn creature finally grasping what is expected of him. The already-quoted and very articulate Albert Finet writes that in the present dialogue Protestants insist on the two cardinal principles of the Reformation: salvation by faith and the sole authority of Scripture. We have no ambition, writes Finet, to have the Catholics accept the Protestant point of view which is a state of permanent reform and search. On the other hand, Finet expresses his conviction that sooner or later the "silly pretension of papal infallibility" will humbly yield to the service of Jesus Christ.

In the United States Protestant leaders accept the changes

brought about by the dialogue and by the Council with the equanimity of those who may now say: "I told you so." Rather than approve, Dr. Albert C. Outler of Southern Methodist University, and Dr. Robert McAffee Brown (Stanford-University) criticize the Church for an incomplete updating and, in the post-Conciliar period, for a "curial backlash."

At any rate, the direction that the dialogue takes *is* confusing. Vatican diplomacy, very correctly, multiplies its efforts at high-level talks, for example with the Archbishop of Canterbury, while warning the faithful that they ought not to expect spectacular successes within their lifetime. Instead of following this eminently reasonable course, the Church-intellectuals behave like ideological agitators, establishing contact with the religious and political extreme left among Protestant Churches. In other words, they disrupt not only the ordinary life of Catholicism, they give away their real intentions by encouraging anarchy among the irresponsible element of Protestantism too. In the United States their sympathy goes to the notoriously left wing National Council of Churches, not to the doctrinally responsible groups. The true face of the dialogue shows itself: it is *not* between Catholics and Protestants, but between the irresponsible elements of both. It is to be feared that the really demoralizing energy is provided by the Catholic side, if for no other reason than because the Roman Church is still regarded as an elder brother, with longer experience and greater wisdom. This is not expressed aloud but is accepted as fact. The scandal is always greater when the one so-far trusted leads the others astray.

What are likely to be the long-range consequences of the Catholic–Protestant dialogue? All the concessions made by Rome on issues like mixed marriages and joint prayer-meetings hardly scratch the surface, and leave doctrinal differences intact. Let us not be afraid of words: these concessions do not amount to more than a public relations job. If they go further, they will come up against the necessity of real decisions: Is Rome willing to dilute Christ's message as she received it and toward which she has a duty to lead all mankind, and leading *back* the Protes-

tants? This problem cannot be talked out of existence by insisting on friendlier relations, interfaith projects, vigils conducted
together for peace and other purposes. Religion is the domain of
absolute commitment even in this relativistic age. No Church
may ever renounce proselytizing, certainly not the Roman
Church, which would deny its *raison d'être* by not following
Christ's command: "Go and teach all nations . . ." [25]

Two possibilities are open for the dialogue if we are willing
to look at it realistically. One is that nothing decisive will happen outside of clearing up some minor problems like greater
Catholic–Protestant cooperation in various communities. Some
enthusiasts among priests will conduct joint services, give communion to non-Catholics, but with no more result than calling
upon themselves the ephemeral attention of the local press.
When our present way of life in closely pressed-together urban
centers will have undergone changes in directions as yet
unforeseeable, these fragile forms of the dialogue will be the first
to vanish since they are not based either on doctrinal foundation
or on people's genuine needs but only on temporarily whipped-
up, volatile emotions.

The second, more serious possibility is the following. As the
Church's central authority continues to decline, sects are likely
to spring up from local initiative, one adopting a particular form
of liturgy, another a set of prayers and ceremonies, yet others a
modified doctrine. Individual priests, upon leaving their state,
may, for complex psychological motives, initiate their own version of religion and gather disciples. The little regard in which
these sects and individuals hold institutions and institutional
frameworks generally, might make them ignore opportunities to
bring their grievances or reform-mindedness to Rome, and might
allow them to maintain a distant and tenuous relationship with

[25] Delegates to a large missionary gathering in Wharton, Illinois, as reported in the *New York Times* (April 15, 1966) warned that "the ecumenical drive toward union is at the expense of doctrine and missionary re-
cruitment." Organic church union, they declared, "has seldom released a
fresh dynamism." Finally: "We declare that our social action must point
man to—not away from—the actual message of the Gospel, and it must not
promote idealistic and unscriptural expectations of absolute solutions to social problems."

the hierarchy. The latter, that is, the bishops, wishing to avoid further troubles, might allow this relationship to go on indefinitely. Not wanting to show up the Church as a restless and authoritarian organization in a society claiming to become increasingly homogeneous and based on consensus, the national conferences of bishops in each country will prefer to dissimulate the grave but not openly scandalous dissensions. And maybe there will be few scandalous dissensions; instead, there might be listless and indifferent parishioners, led by priests and intellectuals in the state of unnoted unorthodoxy, if not outright heresy. There might be in the schools, seminaries, and universities an anarchistic eclecticism; and there might be among bishops a fear lest more popular candidates are elected by tight pressure groups of priests and laymen—when election of bishops will be done by popular vote in the diocese.

On the one hand, then, there might be sects charting their own course that the Church cannot assimilate, on the other hand, the desire to avoid an open schism might prove strong enough for the Church not to intervene and openly condemn. I expressed the opinion in a previous chapter that the structure of the contemporary world: pluralistic society, orientation toward quantitative achievements and efficiency, concentration of the communication media into new feudalisms, and the near-monopoly of the liberal Establishment on opinion-shaping[26]—provides the destroyer of norms and morals with impregnable shelters. Between him (we are speaking now of Catholics) and authority a cushion is formed; newspaper columnists defend the former, panels amplify his complaints and desires; universities discuss and teach his ideas, other Church-intellectuals justify his heretical views. By the time he disappears from the scene (to yield it to one more radical yet), his ideas will have made their

[26] In the December–January 1966–1967 of *The Critic*, publicist John Leo describes the new Liberal Catholic Establishment. It consists of people— publicists, editors, fashionable priest sociologists, columnists—who flatter themselves of being "rebels," but who are in reality, conformists of today's most comfortable and most remunerative rebellion, that against the Church and her tradition. The men mentioned by Mr. Leo, himself included, are typical "Church-intellectuals" of the left and far left in the sense I have been using this term in this chapter.

impact and, given the present uncritical acceptance of novelties which flatter the sentiments and appetites, will have started circulating among like-minded groups.

In such circumstances it is not at all fantastic to speak of a slow Protestantization of the Church, not formally but nevertheless in a penetrating way. If individual and group inspirations overwhelm in number and aggressiveness the authority of the Church, future generations may know a Church still nominally Catholic, but where the inner center of gravity has shifted away from *unity* toward *multiplicity,* and from the equilibrium of faith and reason toward emotions and ideologies. Pluralism in the Church and adaptation to the world, loudly demanded by her intellectuals, lead in straight line to this state of affairs. Thus, indeed, a new Reformation could be prevented, but only at the cost of a disastrous compromise: preserving the outside shell, the institution, but evacuating the content, the truth of Christ.

V

DIALOGUE WITH THE WORLD

We understand the nature of the crisis in the Church when we see her history as the eternal image of Christ being tempted by Satan with domination over the world. Christ rejected this temptation, but it is far more difficult for the Church to do so because it consists of human beings and is implanted in the world through a thousand roots. The temptation, variously formulated throughout history, is called today "dialogue with the world." Semi-officially it is described as a friendly attitude toward, and cooperation with the secularists, Jews, atheists, and Communists,[1] that is, with everybody outside Catholicism. But here again the unstated motives, nuances, and intentions weigh more heavily than what Conciliar documents explicitly contain.

The *world* is defined by the Church-intellectuals as an autonomous entity with its own rules, aspirations, and splendor, in short, as an anti-Church. The pendulum has indeed swung quite the other way since the medieval dispute of the "two swords," temporal and spiritual power. Superiority is now recognized to

[1] Dialogue with Communists is the subject of Chapter VI.

belong to the temporal power, not only to the government but also to the secular principle as such. The Catholic Church must now study the *world* and reformulate her own teachings in the light of what the world reveals as truth. Father Pedro Arrupe, General of the Jesuits, speaks of "the legitimate autonomy of human culture," which would indicate that the Church has abandoned her claim to infuse Christ's truth into the lives of men. Father Arrupe even specifies that it is one particular part of the world, namely the United States, which has taught the Church "to recognize how sacred and central" the two theses are: the equality of all men and their endowment by God with certain unalienable rights.[2]

This statement is obviously mere flattery since it is easily demonstrable that the root of the concept of the sacredness of the person is the monotheistic teaching, and that western political concepts, including those prevailing in the United States, are derived precisely from this religious heritage. But the tendency of Father Arrupe's words is unmistakable: there is no question here of a give-and-take, emphasis is put on the Church's obligation to change and grow in the direction of the world. Texts typical of this obligation abound in the Catholic press: insistence on updating the doctrines according to the latest sociological or psychological data, but never a word about what the *world* might learn from the Church so as to update itself spiritually. Priests are told every day to give up celibacy; never are laymen encouraged to live a chaste life. The Church is asked to introduce the study of Marxism in her seminaries; has any secular school begun studying Catholic theology?

The superiority of the world over the Church is the secular dogma in whose name such one-sidedness and unbalance are taken for granted. This is consistent with the Church-intellectuals' view who, as pantheists, see the universe as having its explanation in itself, not in a transcendant God. The universe, being God, is perfect, except for little specks of impurity here and

2 "The University in the American Experience," speech at Fordham University, April 5, 1966, published by Fordham University, p. 20.

there, gradually eliminated by evolution. All converge toward one ineluctably emerging divinity. The Church may have had her appointed role in this scheme, namely to bring mankind to a point of maturation. But now that this is done, the world takes over, and any insistence on the Church's part that her mission is not yet fulfilled, meets the angry retort that the Church wants to perpetuate her power over the minds of emancipated men.

The French Catholic philosopher, Claude Tresmontant, has some penetrating remarks on this subject. The whole problem is to know, he said to an interviewer,[3] whether the world is an absolute being, the only being. If we recognize that the world, its existence, structure, and history, is not self-sufficient, then our intelligence is freed from the "cosmic idolatry which ascribes to the world the attributes of the absolute being." Therefore the first phase of the knowledge of God is the critique of pantheism in all its forms so evident today, whether these forms are open or hidden.

The Church-intellectual denies, of course, that he is a pantheist. Yet, his genuflections before the world in the name of efficiency and ephemeral achievements (and if not ephemeral, always ambiguous) justify Tresmontant's strictures. In the previous chapter I spoke of the motivations for dialogue with Protestants as being also the admiration for the industrial-technological society built on the Protestant ethos. This admiration for the world's supposed goodness goes, however, beyond this point: it is, indeed, assumed that by and large mankind has solved its great problems. The premise is that we have emerged, particularly after the cataclysm of the Second World War, from the penultimate phase. This is assumed for two reasons, both of them emotionally and intolerantly asserted, therefore unable to stand the scrutiny of reason. The first is that, with Nazism, the greatest evil of which man is capable has been made real and thus defeated; from now on the curve of history may only point upward. The second is that the invention of nuclear weapons,

[3] "Comment se pose aujourd'hui le problème de l'existence de Dieu?" *La France Catholique*, May 20, 1966.

while a horrible thing in itself, will help henceforward to tame man's warring instincts: a limit has been achieved beyond which we cannot go in search of irresponsible adventures.

With the greatest evils thus assumed to have been eliminated, mankind is expected to concentrate its collective efforts on constructive tasks: the first is to become unified under a world government while preserving the plurality that an ideal democratic world structure demands; the second is to constitute a global welfare state so that service should take the place of earlier authoritarian forms.

These utopian expectations form the ground on which the Church-intellectuals, among them serious theologians, try to build a new Church. It is easily seen, however, that the theological trappings form a very thin veil under which nothing more substantial is proposed than what we may hear any day from the lips of publicity-seeking public figures or delegates at the United Nations. Embroidering on the thesis of Jacques Maritain that mankind has entered the age of desacralization, the Church-intellectuals rush to unwarranted conclusions with a zeal worthier of the neophytes of a new faith. We have pointed out in Chapter I that what Maritain is justified in saying (in *Integral Humanism*, *Les Droits de l'homme et la loi naturelle*, and elsewhere) is that the nineteenth and twentieth centuries have witnessed the emergence and spread of secularist societies with an industrial and technological bent. The Promethean man is today the ruling type, and the chief virtue he seeks is efficiency. This is what made German culture historians formulate types like Apollonian and Dionysian, this is Goethe's conclusion in *Faust* ("At the beginning was the Deed," Faust, misled by Mephistopheles, jubilantly exclaims), and this is also the meaning of Nietzsche's cry that "God is dead" and that we must now proceed with the disvaluation of all values.

What is, perhaps, a respectable conceptual game for writers, artists, and historians of culture, cannot form the basis of meditations about Christianity and speculation about the future of the Church. The above formulations and theories are offspring of a historical moment and a sociological mood. Because the Church is eternal, she cannot adapt her program to such a moment and mood, she cannot close the Gospels and open another book. These centuries and the next several may bear out Maritain's or Nietzsche's diagnosis, but the Church, with longer roots and, above all, longer branches than can be measured by centuries, cannot vary her message or reorientate the faith of Christians.

Yet, with an *esprit de sérieux* unworthy of famous theologians, Karl Rahner bases his remarks about the future of the Church on the ephemeral mood of a century. My purpose here is not so much pointing out where he errs, but showing that his "updated" analysis is the exact copy of what a popular minority of Establishment world-affairs analysts say. This absence of originality, together with the falsely profound use of Church terminology, are the best indications that Rahner's diagnosis and prognosis ought not to be taken too seriously. It is proof also of the falseness of the dialogue pretense, since Rahner merely lends the name and reputation of a theologian to a mundane view of the Church, the world, and their expected relationship.

Karl Rahner, as also Fathers, Küng, Liégé, Chenu, and many others accept with the sociologist's single-mindedness the fact of de-Christianization. It is hard to decide whether they see this situation exclusively through the eyes of pollsters and commentators to whose views they pay such an exaggerated tribute, or whether they are anguished beyond the sociologist's interest in data. But by all evidence they are *not* overanxious to become prophets in the Old Testament sense, calling the people sinful, and in the face of "scientific" research data, thundering against godlessness. This obviously seems to them an attitude smacking of triumphalism.

My suspicion is that they welcome the present situation with the masochism characteristic of certain members of western intelligentsia vis-à-vis nonwesterners, of Catholics vis-à-vis non-Catholics, of white men vis-à-vis nonwhites, and so on.

Rahner, for example, tells Catholics not to regard the present "diaspora" situation as a misfortune; the fact that Christianity was dominant for fifteen hundred years was a historical coincidence which left the Church with bad habits, absolutism, triumphalism, militancy. The diaspora is not a disaster but a "preordained must in the history of salvation." [4]

A few comments are in order. We do not know of any diaspora except the willed dispersion ending in general demoralization that the Church-intellectuals themselves have brought about. The method is notorious and could be described, somewhat crudely, as letting rats loose in a dwelling, then lamenting that the place has become uninhabitable. It seems then like a reasonable recommendation to burn down the house, unless we choose to share it with the rats. Secondly, there was no preordained diaspora "necessary for salvation"; this is not theological but Hegelian-Marxist language, as when the bourgeois class is told that proletarian dictatorship is willed by history for mankind's social salvation.

Indeed, this is the reasoning that Rahner admits between the lines. The diaspora seems to have been a deserved punishment because Christians have lived in a ghetto, although "as everybody knows [?], only certain sociological and cultural types feel comfortable in a ghetto." Who are they? "In our case, the petty bourgeois in contrast to the worker of today or the man of tomorrow's atomic age. . . . The Church is cluttered up with pseudo-Gothic decor and other kinds of reactionary petty-bourgeois stuff." [5]

It is a sad but also irresistibly grotesque thing to read under the pen of ultra-modern theologians all the warmed-up terms so popular in Marxist literature of some decades ago. As with sex, so with Marxism, our Church-intellectuals wax positively enthusiastic. I remember from my adolescent years that smoking and talk of sex were the signs of emancipation. Father Rahner must think of himself as a man of the world when, authorized by the *Zeitgeist*, he utters words taken from the dusty arsenal of Marx-

4 *The Christian Commitment*, p. 27.
5 *Idem*, p. 30.

ism—words that a Brezhnev would use today only for external consumption.[6]

It would be easy to dismiss Rahner's words about the diaspora and the ghetto as derived from sociological data which, like all sociological data, are, to say the least, controvertible. However, the trouble with Church-intellectuals like Rahner is that they add an unmistakably religious dimension to the profanest and most trivial notions they use. For instead of merely analyzing the diaspora and also merely analyzing the milieu outside the "ghetto," he laments like a Jeremiah over the former and writes with a misplaced finality about the latter. The world, under his pen, becomes a frighteningly compact entity before which the Christian's only reaction may be awe: the world of the purely profane has today "a density, an inevitability, an almost total impenetrability" which simply have to be realistically accepted by Christians. This is again Karl Rahner's Hegelian inspiration and Heideggerian discipleship, for the Jewish prophets never advised Israel to "realistically accept" the world's turning away from God and toward material idols like Rahner's "impenetrable profane world."

But Rahner is irrevocably impressed by this modern idol, although, as I said before, the pattern of his impressionability is distressingly unoriginal. He accepts and approves the growing power of the centralized State, and notes at the same time that a "new entity is forced into existence . . . the State or the community of peoples organized at a planetary level." [7] In face of this obviously secular Leviathan "it is useless to commend our Christian principles to the world as its salvation. What it [the

[6] Note the similarity between Rahner's full-mouthed use of Marxist rhetoric and Father Congar's anxious flattery of the "masses": "Conservatives," Congar wrote, "are anti-people, anti-mass; they react inimically to everything favoring the masses: paid vacations, worker-priests, the vernacular in the liturgy, and the easier access to education." (In *Informations Catholiques Internationales*, September 15, 1965.) I would not be surprised to hear that labor union men would indignantly reject Congar's style in writing of masses, particularly his Marxist assumption that "working men" form one indistinguishable category with uniform views about worker-priests, vernacular, and education.

[7] *The Christian Commitment*, p. 13.

world] wants to hear is concrete proposals. We have got to have the courage to act as human beings with a task in the world of history, and so to come forward with such proposals. But we cannot propagate them in the name of Christianity." [8] We note again the excruciating degree of bad faith; in another of his books,[9] Rahner states with a detachment seemingly dictated by regretful resignation, but hiding, in fact, a sense of satisfaction, that whenever a form of the Church's influence disappears *against our own will and despite all we do* (my italics), we are still far from being lost because we may regain this influence in different ways. But, we ask, why should we lose this influence in the first place if we judge it beneficial for the world?—and why should we regain it if it was not beneficial? The only explanation, given today with monotonous uniformity by these Church-intellectuals, is that the world must be shared (so as to avoid a nuclear confrontation, we assume) by many different ideologies, therefore the Church, as Hans Küng writes, should not try to conquer the world but "serve mankind." He adds: "God's victory need not always be the victory of the Church." [10]

All these arguments amount to a dissociation of the Church and man's spiritual destiny. It is not denied (nor is it affirmed) that the Church leads man to salvation, but a different, a temporal and secular priority is consistently observed: the task is to propose to mankind what it seems to want, and *not* to propose it in the name of Christianity. Nothing could be more inexorably anti-Christian than this new priority. Not only are its criteria invariably collectivistic with large streaks of hardly hidden Marxism in them, but they are collectivistic because the Church-intellectuals have transferred the attributes of God to society. How else could a Teilhard de Chardin be so uncharitable (by Christian standards) as to belittle the sacrifice of millions—in Hitlerist and Communist concentration camps and at Hiroshima—in

---

[8] *Idem*, p. 11.

[9] *Free Speech in the Church*, p. 88.

[10] Echoed by Rahner: "We should not sigh and say: 'We are up to 17 per cent.' Just where is it written that *we* must have the whole 100 per cent? God must have all . . . But we cannot say that he is doing so only if we, meaning the Church, have everybody." *The Christian Commitment*, p. 35.

the name of what he called "increasing hominization" of the evolutionary material? How else can Rahner say that "one real conversion in a great city is something more splendid than the spectacle of a whole remote village going to the sacraments. The one is an essentially religious event, a thing of grace; the other is to a large extent a sociological phenomenon, even though it may be a means of God's grace." [11]

Teilhard's words originate in his conviction that man's ultimate allegiance is not to God but to the world, the initial matter constantly refined and spiritualized until a "cosmic Christ" emerges at the end of evolution, in Omega Point. Although a good priest, he admitted: "If I lost my faith in Christ, in a personal God, in the Holy Ghost, I would still continue believing in the World. The first and last thing I believe in is the value, the infallibility and the goodness of the World. In the moment of my death it is to this faith that I shall abandon myself." [12] Teilhard's philosophy may be misunderstood by many Catholics who would turn away from it once they become better informed, but it authorizes in the meantime all the vague declarations of love to the world as it is or is expected to become. It serves admirably the purposes of contemporary collectivistic ideologies because it is willfully blind to evil, judging it to be a remnant of materiality in the evolutionary process gradually cleared away by an increasing spiritualization of matter. Hence Father Teilhard's just mentioned scandalous statement about the relative insignificance of concrete forms of suffering in view of mankind's cosmic adventure. What is this if not an unreasoning confidence in the world as an autonomous and self-regulating mechanism?

In a more prosaic manner, Karl Rahner too shows himself as an adept of modern sociology with its centeredness on the urban mode of life. Like Teilhard, he too is lacking in charity when he dismisses village piety as part of folklore. This reduces to size our Church-intellectuals' grandiloquent statements about the "world"; in their stale sociological categories the "world"

---

[11] *The Christian Commitment*, p. 33.
[12] In *Comment je crois* (1934).

becomes city life with its intellectual coffee-klatches. Father
Jean Daniélou wrote a pertinent critique of this un-Christian
contempt for what is now called "popular forms of Christianity"
in contrast to "cultural" forms. By what right do we minimize
and deprecate a religiosity which consists of confiding to God
our everyday worries? asks Father Daniélou.[13] This is the most
genuine expression of religion as a relationship with God. An
old woman placing a candle on the Virgin's altar because a child
is ill accomplishes a truly religious act. "The ways of approach-
ing God are diverse, and those of Christian people are worthy of
an immense respect."

The Daniélou text points admirably to the limitations of
the "dialogue with the world" which is, in the first place, not a
dialogue but an uncritical surrender, and, in the second place, a
surrender to one particular manifestation of the world with the
exclusion of others. Through this supposed dialogue Church-
intellectuals speak with their fellow intellectuals outside the
Church, the first genuflecting to the values of the second, and
thus bringing nothing more to the dialogue than a secret urge to
destroy their own spiritual home. The result is a strange but
quite natural desiccation of the efficiency sought with an almost
otherworldly greed. I could observe this in Latin America where
a large segment of the clergy and what I call the Church-intellectuals are in the process of canceling out their efficacy as
priests and as Catholics, without being able to fill the vacuum as
sociologists. The most unreliable information I gathered while
visiting the various countries of the continent had priests as
sources. They take their own impatience and revolutionary fer-
vor for guarantee of social betterment, their zeal for competence, their denunciations of injustice for dispassionate analysis.
The remedies they propose are quaintly out or piac- and show
bookish learning, the slogans they adopt are at once exploited by
anti-Catholic agitators, the statements they issue contribute not
to the elaboration of reasonable guidelines but to social restless-
ness and a sense of despair. As one of their critics, the Brazilian
writer Gustavo Corsaõ, pointed out, prelates should give spirit-

[13] *Bulletin Saint Jean Baptiste,* October–November 1966.

ual guidance but not discuss, since it is not within their competence, the yield of milk per cow.

The last remark which seems like an exaggerated satire may serve as a symbol for the "age of the dialogue": it signifies that the Church, or anyway a vocal minority claiming to speak for her, has ceased performing the tasks for which she was appointed by her divine teacher. She, or they, put now the religious energy and the institutional mechanism at the disposal of this energy, to ill-defined, ad hoc uses, labeled mostly: help to the world or service to the world. Churchmen, confused but probably happy to see themselves and the Church in the news after centuries of "bad press," do not seem to have the courage and the strength to face obscurity and unpopularity once again.[14] Rather, they adapt themselves with surprising ease to the age of public relations, and appear to believe that even being badly spoken of is better than neglect. I fear that what they call "to be in the world" is, in reality, "to be in the news."

Indeed, the Church ought to be at all times in the world. Yet, I tried to show on the preceding pages that the Church-intellectuals have carved out for specially favored treatment a small segment of today's world, the urban-industrial segment. In this they imitate the Marxists who are similarly obsessed with industrialization and urban structure of life. Rahner's contempt for the piety of peasants—"one would almost like to say folk-costume Christianity," he writes—echoes Nikita Khrushchev's insistence on settling them in *agrovilles* and put agriculture on a compulsory industrial-production basis. When Fathers Houtart and Pin report on the state of religion in Latin America,[15] they treat Christianity purely as a sociological phenomenon, as if it consisted of the listing and description of classes, types, and categories, and not even marginally of the salvation of souls. The

[14] Jean Guitton mentions that at least one reason why Teilhard stressed the worldly involvement (which he called "horizontal") above the soul's relationship to God (the "vertical") was to dispel the general impression that Christians undervalue the world, progress, the techniques and the material aspects of existence.

[15] *The Church and the Latin American Revolution* (New York, Sheed & Ward, 1966).

whole emphasis in this and numerous other books by "updating" authors strikes the reader with a kind of long-chewed, bitter tone, the slavish repetition of conclusions reached by the most revolutionary, antireligious authors.

Industry, technology, and city life are, however, not the only privileged sectors the Church-intellectuals select for dialoguing. Their general rush for acceptance by the modern world does not take place without their sharp-eyed discernment of who are the powerful and the influential of this world. This is partly dictated by opportunism, but opportunism itself can only be effective if those in the frontline of the dialogue naturally speak and think the way their partners on the other side do. The dialogue is not, then, a mere tactics; it is the sign that certain people are trying to conquer the Church from inside by stressing the need for good public relations, deemphasizing doctrine, saying the popular things, allying themselves with the world in order to suppress the traditional element in the Church.

Father Yves Congar was right when, commenting on the *aggiornamento* of the Church, he said we were living through the Church's "October Revolution." The Church-intellectuals like and often use the term "revolution," although they may want also to preserve a kind of continuity in the Church (like the Bolsheviks in 1917 who also worked and fought in the historical framework of Russia). Yet, the creation of the Soviet Union, at least in the minds of Communists, was not to give rise to a clearly identifiable country and nation, it was to be merely the base of the world revolution, a base to which other revolutionary units (previously called "countries") were to be added until the final form, the World Classless Society, will have been established. If this did not come to pass, and if its historical realization has receded beyond the horizon of revolutionary hopes (although *not* of revolutionary slogans), more powerful factors even than ideologies are responsible. The same thing will happen in the present crisis: the Church's continuity, guaranteed by the greatest spiritual power, will be preserved. But her intellectuals do envisage, as we have seen, a Church wider than the Catholic Church, encompassing the world and grouping all religions, ideologies, beliefs, and convictions. In the process of emergence, this World Church is supposed to absorb much of what its constituting elements contain but even more of this content is to be jettisoned. Viewed by the Church-intellectuals, the Catholic Church must make the greatest sacrifices: renouncing her personality and beliefs. These men see only one aspect of the Church which they call, without understanding it, *love*. And love for them begins when the personality ends since the mere assertion of the self appears to them as the root of selfishness. What they call "triumphalism" is this self-affirmation of the Church, whether her efforts to proselytize or her incorporation of splendor and ceremony into her liturgical life.

It is then entirely logical that the main object of modernization and radical alteration, indeed destruction, is the Catholic Church, this strange human institution with roots in the supernatural, a unique obstacle in the way of the World Church (or United Religions Organization, as it is already called in imitation of the United Nations Organization). The Church-intellectuals will feel frustrated and embarrassed as long as the Church in her present form continues to exist because, reinterpreting Christ's teaching, they do not want to wait until all men become converted to Christ, but urge Catholics to use their spiritual energy, a reconverted energy, as contribution to a more "catholic" and successful World Church. Hence the earlier quoted statements by Rahner, Teilhard de Chardin, Küng, and others who are settling down not spiritually distressed but spiritually comforted by the fact that "since the world religions are not bound to disappear, one cannot talk to mankind from Rome." (Hans Küng).

The World Church which would hardly be as Catholic, or for that matter believing in God, is a kind of utopian fantasy often indulged in by various thinkers throughout the ages. It belongs to the literature of utopia, and its logical end, never to be tested in history, would be the most absolute rule ever experienced on earth, the combination of temporal and spiritual powers. At present, however, it is quite consistent with the Church ideologues' orientation to strengthen through the dialogue the forces whose main ideological thrust is in the direction of a World Church.

Let us be clear about this. We do not speak here of a formally constituted World Church. Various ages toyed with the concept, either in the form of a syncretistic religion (in the Hellenistic age and in the Age of Enlightenment, for example Lessing in *Nathan the Wise*, then again Auguste Comte with his positivistic religion), or as a symbol of religious tolerance. Today, in the age of the United Nations, we hear again syncretist statements, but not so much as a proposal for a new faith for all in Christ or Moses, Mohammed, Confucius, or Buddha, as a secular ideology collectively adopted, a way of neutralizing the existing religions. In this sense the World Church is really its opposite: no Church at all, only welfare agencies of a vaguely ethical character.

Outside the dialogue with Protestants, justifiable also on firmer grounds than the one claimed by Church-intellectuals, there is then another set of dialogues with Jews and atheists representing "the world." Why are Jews and atheists the par excellence representatives of the world in the eyes of Church-intellectuals?

One guideline to the latter's behavior is that in every conceivable situation they take a position contrary to that of the Church. The Church maintains that a tremendous mystery is involved in the role the Jews played around the Crucifixion, and that, as God's chosen people, the consummation of times will come with their conversion only. The Jews hold, on the other hand, that the appearance of Jesus was an untoward, blasphemous incident in the history of Judaism, and that the Church, an institution founded on mistaken beliefs (properly a heresy), served to crystalize and promote anti-Semitism wherever it commended spiritual loyalties.

It is evident that these two views are irreconcilable and will be opposed till the end of times. Like between Catholics and Protestants, but far more essentially, the theses of Catholics and

Jews embody, one the concept of hope fulfilled, the other of hope open; one the concept of salvation through Christ, the other of a renewed Jerusalem where, in the words of the Psalmist, "the nations may come from the ends of the earth to see his [the Messiah's] glory." [16]

Dialogue, while always possible and commendable between persons and groups, is a sham solution on a doctrinal level. Its Catholic partisans can always claim, like many Jews, that anti-Semitism is a Christian invention and a Christian crime, and that therefore only an endless and sincere contrition may atone for it. But this position does not rest on any firm ground, theological or historical, and its affirmation serves merely to accredit the similarly false view that the exacerbated anti-Semitism of the Hitler era was of a Christian inspiration.

However, the role of the Jews as Hitler's par excellence victims has catapulated them, by an understandable rebound, into the role of ideological inspirers and articulators of the postwar world. This, and not philo-Semitism, explains the undignified excesses of Catholic intellectuals in flattering the Jews and extending to them an offer of "dialogue," a dialogue which, like the others, is destined to fade with the years. But note the difference: the Church, through her doctors and popes, recognizes Israel as carrier of God's special message to mankind, and as the source of Christianity. Recent popes spoke of Christians as "spiritually Jewish." It is the destiny of Israel under God before which the Church bows her head. Whereas the Church-intellectuals see in Jews princes of the desacralized world, a pressure group flattered for what it is expected to do for the desacralization of the Church. This point is deeply understood and brilliantly expressed by Manes Sperber when he writes of the Jews' "disidentification." In the past, he writes, when they were persecuted, the Jews died for their faith and for God. The Hitlerist persecution found them, as well as their assassins, devoid of any religion; desacralized and disintegrated, they died for nothing, at the hands of brutal men who killed not in the name of Christ but as unmotivated murderers.

[16] Psalms of Solomon, XVII.

The dialoguers' attitude vis-à-vis the Jews is the exact copy of their attitude vis-à-vis the Protestants: dialogue is established only with certain branches of Judaism, not with others; with dereligionized, not orthodox Jews; with Jews for whom religion is not much more than social welfare plus a drop of ethical perfume, not with Jews who live an intense religious life under the jealous eyes of Jahweh. In other words, the Church-intellectuals act not only in their own Church but also in other religious communities as dissolvants of faith. Because not only is the Catholic Church defined spiritually as the mystical body of Christ in which all are accountable for all others; the religions of mankind too form a mysterious spiritual community where weakening at any point reverberates on the destiny of the whole. Any such act of weakening ultimately strengthens the Leviathan, another term for the World, the secularist's eternal object of worship.[17]

In view of these considerations it is pitiful to behold the stampede of Church-intellectuals onto the necessarily fragile bridge of the dialogue. The award for the triviality in flattery goes perhaps to Father John B. Sheerin who, as reported by *The New York Times* (May 24, 1966), called for a new name for the Old Testament since "old" must be insulting to Jews. A nun in the audience where this statement was made suggested "Jewish Scripture." Finally a rabbi put an end to this distasteful game by tactfully reminding the Catholic dialoguers that since the Old Testament is a Jewish work, the Jews might be permitted to select a name for it without the zealous help of others.[18]

[17] A most interesting debate on the pages of *Commentary*, the American Jewish magazine, between Ivan Shapiro and Milton Himmelfarb, illustrated this point sharply (December 1966). Against Shapiro's fervid arguments for total separation of Church and State, Himmelfarb, with cogent reasoning and fine irony, pointed out that if such a separation were indeed total, our schools (education was at the core of the debate) would never inculcate the moral ideals, to speak of nothing else, by which a secular State too must live if it wants to survive and not be submerged in licentiousness and anarchy. If our schools do not allow or encourage the taking of marijuana in spite of the student-citizens' right to indulge in drugs, this is because religious doctrine (Christian or Judeo-Christian) forbids it in the name of ethical norms that these religions derive from divine commandments.

[18] An even more ludicrous example of this kind was the proposal by a

The dialoguers claim that this kind of thing forms part of a rapprochement with Judaism. Are they sure that the Jews on the other end of the dialogue-bridge welcome it, take it at its face value, and will in any sense be changed by it? The evidence, more, even, than in the case of the Protestants, point to the contrary.

First of all, one might say with a measure of truth that, in proportion as the Catholic Church seems to beat an ever-louder *mea culpa*, the other religions in spiritual kinship with her become more triumphalist. This is a reasonable perspective since they conclude that in the subtle and unspoken but nevertheless real contest—between Catholics and Protestants and between Christians and Jews—the non-Catholic side is winning. Catholicism is weakening, they say, when the so-powerful central inspiration is dispersed by its own personnel. Or, they may believe that Catholicism passes, indeed, through a crisis, but wants to recoup her fortunes by an adroit strategy, the kind known as mimicry in the animal kingdom: by pretending to be like any other religion. Catholicism tries to put to sleep age-old suspicions that it claims superiority and seeks power.

Historically, Judaism has always been a "triumphalist" religion. Jews denounced and persecuted the early Christians in the Roman Empire because of the scandal that Christ and his teaching represented in the eyes of Jewish communities. Even before the birth of Jesus this triumphalism stands out with a vibrant faith and self-confidence on every page of the Bible, even when Israel is chastized by God. After all, only the sons are worthy of the Father's wrath. The triumph will be complete at the coming of the Messiah: "He shall destroy the ungodly nations with the word of his mouth . . . He shall possess the nations of the heathen to serve him beneath his yoke." [19]

The same reaction is evident in responsible Jewish circles in the face of the Catholic dialogue makers. In a very interesting

---

Protestant minister, Doctor Palen, to drop worship on Sunday and switch to Saturday as a show of good will toward Jews.

[19] Psalms of Solomon, XVII, 27–33.

article some time ago, Professor Eliezer Berkovits[20] examined the meaning of the Church's *aggiornamento*. One sign that the Christian era has come to an end, writes Professor Berkovits, is that other ideologies have become as aggressive as Christianity used to be. Note that the author is not afraid to identify the exhaustion of a spiritual belief with the diminution of its aggressiveness, that is, self-assertion, appetite for expansion, confidence in its own exclusive truth, and will to proselytize. Ecumenism, according to this diagnosis, is then a sign of weakness, the grabbing of the last straw, the reaching for the arms of earlier opponents. But why should these earlier opponents accept the extended arm? Why should Jews become "ecumenical"? Not only that Jews should not lend themselves to this dubious attempt of "whitewashing [the Church's] criminal past," they should stay away from the dialogue altogether lest they become doctrinally weakened. The Jews, as "eternal witnesses of history," should merely wait until Christianity too vanishes, as have vanished their former persecutors, Assyrians, Syrians, or Romans. They will survive into the post-Christian era.

Similar points were raised by Rabbi Zev Segal of Newark[21] before the Rabbinical Council representing United States and Canadian rabbis. He too attacked the concept of "homogenized" religion, the likely outcrop of interfaith dialogues on other than large social issues. "Discussion of the deep religious commitments which a faith community holds can only serve to confuse," he warned. "There is a particular relationship between man and his God that is not subject to either debate or persuasion." Significantly, at a time when Church-intellectuals scorn the teaching authority of the Church and set themselves up as fullfledged spokesmen in doctrinal issues, Rabbi Segal had the courage to assert with respect to Jews that leaders of secular organizations are "incompetent and unqualified" to undertake in-

[20] "Judaism in the Post-Christian Era," *Judaism*, a publication by the Hebrew Union College, Skokie, Ill.
[21] *The New York Times*, Jan. 31, 1967.

terfaith religious dialogues. Such discussions, he said, "are damaging because they undermine religious commitments."

The not-so-tacit conclusion of both Berkovits and Segal is that whatever the future of the Catholic Church might be—and this is obviously not their main concern—the Catholic dialoguer's activity is in the direction of weakening man's religious commitments. What one terms "confusion" and the other "post-Christian" era is, in reality, the World Church, the religious no-man's-land if we state it negatively, but positively stated it is the planetwide secularist theocracy, persecutor of Christian and Jew alike. Hence the Church-intellectual's real aim is dialogue with atheism for which the one with the Jews represents a convenient passageway.

Atheism might seem easy to define as simply absence of belief in God. But atheists do not like this definition which presupposes God's existence and points to certain people who almost by caprice, reject this existence. Whatever definition we choose, it must be obvious that we do not speak of mere indifference or lack of stimulation to speak about things divine, but of militant atheism which, pretexting the *fact* of churches (organized religion), attacks religion as a misconstrued view of the world or as a sociological remnant of the past. In the last hundred years or so militant atheists were such men as Feuerbach, Comte, Marx, Nietzsche, Bertrand Russell, Sartre, and the like. All may be grouped as "radical humanists," that is, not only negators of a personal God, but also affirmers of the exclusiveness of man as shaper and judge of his destiny.

It needs no special emphasis, as is the fashion today in the Church-conducted advertising campaigns, that the Church must at all times concern herself with teaching the truth and converting souls. And this must be done with those outside the Church even more than with those inside: the shepherd goes after the lost sheep even while leaving his flock (although without ridiculing the latter's fidelity as Rahner does). It is worth noting that in the last century when the Church lived supposedly in the "ghetto" and at a time when Pius IX condemned the tenets of modernism, there were more distinguished converts to Catholicism than in our own mid-century when the Church, hard-pressed by her intellectuals, tries, so to speak, to disappear in the crowd.[22] Converts come to the Church not because they find correct sociological or economic theories expounded from the pulpit and in encyclicals, but because they fathom her spiritual depth and are enveloped in her charity. That is when, as Professor Berkovits clearly perceived, the Church's faith in her mission is vigorous and unquestioning.

The Church does not have to be reminded of her need of converts, that is, of the essential necessity for her to remain the teacher of mankind, including the nonbelievers and the atheists. We criticize the dialogue on these pages precisely because we see in it the opposite of the teaching magisterium: subservience to the world's dictates, the betrayal of those who want to be taught. Are they atheists? Hardly. They form a great, an infinite variety of people, as richly diverse as mankind itself. They, like Plato's cave dwellers, live immersed in the world which is our natural condition, but they live there deprived of certain moral encouragements. Since their natural lights tell them where these encouragements would lead, people are torn between a desire for a less exclusively mundane condition and a resistance to this desire. The result is that they are embarrassed by their own secret hopes. They are embarrassed because others, with a basically similar conflict within them, would mock their efforts to change. And change, that is, conversion, becomes then twice as hard. Yet these are the people whom the Church must ceaselessly seek out because they hide in the hope of being found.[23] What makes them hide and hesitate is, surprisingly, but happily, the fear of scandal, a strong motivation which testifies for moral health in no matter what circumstances. In this case it is the scandal of a milieu unfavorable to conversion, the desacral-

22 A few names should be mentioned: John Henry Newman, Paul Claudel, Edith Stein, Karl-Joris Huysmans, Jacques Maritain, etc.

23 The spiritual road of Simone Weil and of Edith Stein comes here to mind as an illustration.

ized milieu. The Church must respect this fear of scandal but must also gently show that it would be a greater scandal to offend God and make Him wait at the threshold.

But there is another scandal, greater yet (if we may speak of degrees in this matter). It consists of the dialogue the Church-intellectuals urge the Church to conduct with atheists. It is scandalous because it blocks a hope by showing respect for the state of atheism from which the hiding soul wishes to emerge. It throws him back as one might do with a drowning man whose reaching hands the safe ones inside the lifeboat cruelly push away. The atheist is not a man who, by dint of superior intellectual powers, formulates the objections of others against the existence of God. It is a mistake to assume that if the Church succeeds (a self-contradictory assumption) in reaching a *modus vivendi* with Feuerbach, Marx, or Sartre, then masses of converts will join her. They will be merely bewildered and demoralized because their secret hope was precisely to escape from the arguments and moral ascendancy of Feuerbach, Marx, or Sartre.

It is, I hope, clear that these names are not mentioned here in order to designate certain individuals as possible converts; in our context Feuerbach, etc., represent virulent and muscle-flexing atheism with which, as Cardinal Franciscus Koenig wrote (in the Catholic weekly, *Echo der Zeit*), reconciliation on religious or theological grounds cannot come. Is it also impossible intellectually?

What is "inconvertible" in atheism is not the denial of God, it is the divinization of man. Heresies in the course of Church history mistook the call of Christianity for purity as an invitation to be Godlike, all-pure,[24] all-knowing, all-mighty. In our own time this temptation is reinforced by science and the technological advances it helped achieve, so that man's own power, and his feeling of power, make him think of himself as self-sufficient, Godlike. This is why I spoke above of "muscle-

---

[24] Total purity was interpreted by the Cathars, for example, as abstinence from marriage and suicide by slow starvation so as to liberate the soul from the prison of the flesh.

flexing" atheism, although it is important to realize that it is of
the same essence as earlier forms when spiritual, not technological pride was at its surface. But of course atheism always ends up
in spiritual pride which, in turn, leads to absolute license; in the
words of Dostoevsky's hero Kirilov: If God does not exist, everything is permitted. Thus an inner logic is at work when our
Church-intellectuals who begin by taking apart the doctrine, invariably end up encouraging unrestrained sexual indulgence.
Complete license, in mankind's moral history, has always
meant: free and unlimited sex.

The main intellectual thrust of modern atheism is the
claim that God is man's invention, and that if he emancipates
himself from oppressive material conditions, the need to project
a divine absolute outside himself will vanish. Man will then re-
absorb the divine attributes which in reality belong to him. This
process is promoted by science, psychology, and the political re-
organization of the earth. The thesis is so persuasive that even
such a self-asserting thinker as J. P. Sartre subordinates his existentialism to it by recognizing the epoch-shaping superiority of
Marxism. What we have then before us in contemporary humanism is not a speculative fragment but a human "theodicy":
a discourse about man *as* God.

It is understandable that the Catholic doctrine cannot
"bite" on this system which, in a religiously permeated age,
would be called "heresy." Its superficial optimism (preserved
until its ruthlessness begins to show) makes it popular because
the unlimited perspective of human power before which it places
us appeals to our love of adventure and Promethean inclinations. When a Father François Biot, indignant that Maritain
dare criticize the lucubrations of Teilhard de Chardin, calls us,
obviously in the name of Teilhardism, "to live today's adventure
with the world," [25] (a phrase rather reminiscent of the fascist
"Let's live dangerously!"), we detect behind the vacuity of the
call the idolatry of power, the diffuse emotional response to
technical accomplishments. For, after all, space flight and moon

[25] *Témoignage Chretien*, December 15, 1966.

landing require no theological readjustment to be valid human enterprises, and Maritain's critique of Teilhard must be judged on the merits of his arguments, not as a declaration for or against technological accomplishments.

Does Catholic doctrine have a better chance of dialoguing with the pessimistic variety of contemporary atheism? This variety is related to the "God is dead" mood, or, at least, seems to be nostalgic for an absolute which either cannot exist or has ceased to exist. Representatives of this mood seem indeed to hold that although God was a powerful *idea* influencing the destinies of many former generations, today this source of inspiration is found to be mythical. These pseudo-theologians, morally and metaphysically weak-kneed, always end up joining the secular city; their lament over God's death is only an intriguing detour to reach a foregone conclusion. But their pessimism and despair are not feigned; they could say with Sartre that "nothing, absolutely nothing can justify my adopting this or that value." [26] But in their eyes not only values have no foundation in reality, human existence itself is devoid of "thickness" (*épaisseur*), as they say in the Sartrian jargon.

Now this entire philosophy of the absurd of which the "God is dead" movement is only an offshoot, is a systematic discreditation of life, existence itself, consciousness, ethical norms, even of coherence in language. It is based on a totally pessimistic analysis of the human condition. Man's passion, Hegel, Marx, Sartre, Camus, etc., hold, is to achieve absolute freedom, the combination of the subjective and the objective, so that man may lose himself as man and "God may come to life." [27] Yet, this alleged project too is futile: "We lose ourselves in vain. Man is a useless passion." [28]

Professor Albert Dondeyne of Louvain comments with laudable common sense that such a passion does not exist at all, and that when Saint Thomas tells us that there is within us a

[26] *L'Être et le Néant* (Paris, Gallimard, 1943), p. 76.
[27] *Idem*, p. 708.
[28] *Idem*, p. 708.

natural desire for God, he does not mean that we desire to become God but only to encounter Him.[29] Yet, the impossibility
to satisfy this pseudo-desire is sufficient to level a flat condemnation against God, human existence, and its values, and devise an
abstract "humanism" whose avowed essence is meaninglessness.
Sartre's freedom is, then, simply lack of existence, therefore also
lack of relationships and communication. It is a most inexorably
closed system of thought, opened arbitrarily at one end in the
direction of Marxism,[30] and flowing at the other end—much
more logically—into the Buddhist nirvana of self-annihilation.

In contrast to pessimistic atheism, Christian faith is a
loudly positive response to life. The superiority of contemplative
life does not mean the negation of the practical and worldly,
only the recognition that God has ordered his creation and that
he must be served by all. Work, improvement, curiosity, progress, all are sanctified in the Benedictine synthesis, *ora et labora*.
Life is not to be pedantically venerated as by the Buddhists, who
step carefully for fear of crushing an insect, but preserved in
view of further creation. After all, in the present controversy
about birth control the secular humanists are the misers worried
lest their standard of living is challenged, and the Church takes
the bold view of increasing productivity, both of human lives
and of foodstuffs to sustain them.

Over against this positive answer to life (*Bejahung*), Buddhism which inspires our humanists and absurdists, is the very
principle of negation. Buddhists pass the water they drink
through a sieve so as to spare the microscopic creatues therein;
but this is done because the individual, wandering through many
life forms, may have landed in one of these microbes. And wandering itself—metempsychosis—is a desperate attempt to get rid
of the *élan vital*, of the "yes" to life. While Christian saints
were dynamic men and women of action (Saint Francis, Saint
Theresa of Avila, Saint Catherine of Siena, Saint Ignatius, etc.),

[29] *Contemporary European Thought and Christian Faith* (Pittsburgh,
Duquesne University Press, 1963), pp. 162–63.
[30] "What makes the richness and force of Marxism is that it is the most
radical attempt to shed light on the historical process in its totality."
Critique de la raison dialectique (Paris, Gallimard, 1960), p. 29.

the Buddhist sage lives a process of suppressing all contact with life except that of instructing disciples to do likewise. If life in their conception is not absurd as in the systems of our humanists, it is not because the Oriental sage trusts reason any more than does Sartre, or because he accepts a divine transcendance, or believes in sin; it is because for him "man is defined by the qualities of his heart, by the ethical life, by intuition." [31]

But for the Oriental, like for Sartre, Camus, and Heidegger, the world is unreal, and the ethical life is, at best, lived, not justified. Truth has no meaning, and no meaning is sought for it because finding truth may be frightening: perhaps man is only an anguished animal, haunted by an inexorable enemy, the principle of life. Note: not by Satan, the ensnarer toward death, but by life. No wonder that, as M. Heinrichs remarks, nothingness (*néant*) for the Oriental does not spell terror but trust. If life and procreation are ever-renewed horrors, as in Buddhism, then the only consolation may indeed be that at the end of our wandering the aggregate of atoms we are, will disintegrate. How far is this will to be absorbed in nirvana from the glorious reassurance: *Ego sum via, veritas et vita!*

31 Maurus Heinrichs, *Théologie catholique et pensée asiatique* (Paris, Casterman, 1965), pp. 18, 21, 174.

VI

DIALOGUE WITH
MARXISM

Of all the dialogues now being conducted by official and unofficial representatives of the Catholic Church the one with communism is the most sensationally presented and exploited for its news value. The ecumenical dialogue is a natural process for it is a scandal that there is no unity of doctrine and worship under the name of Christ. Dialogue with the "world," although it includes men of other religions and with no religion, is too vague a notion to be duly noted, except when events like the pope's visit to the United Nations dramatize it. But dialogue with Communists not only intrigues newspaper readers, it also tends to upset, at least on the surface, the various ideological categories into which the intellectual-political life of this century is boxed.

From the Church's point of view (the only one which is of interest to this book), several important remarks are in order. Various popes have warned Catholics that socialism, with its materialism and earth-centeredness, is contrary to Catholic doctrine because it believes in the solution of all problems through a purely economic restructuralization of the world. True, the Socialists, including the direct disciples of Marx, claim that once the chains of economic exploitation are broken, man will be emancipated and promoted to the status of a full human being, and will be able to make use of all his potentials. But this fullness is described as emancipation from all previous alienations of which religion is the most important one and also the last, the hardest to destroy. Indeed, the chief representatives of modern atheism, Feuerbach, Marx, Engels, Auguste Comte, and Nietzsche, saw in one particular religion, Christianity, the most accomplished religion in the sense that it is the one which alienates man most completely: through it, man is lifted, as it were, into another, spiritual world, a world parallel to this one, but forming a system in and by itself. Hence the Marxist attack against religion concentrates on Christianity; if the latter can be smashed, then man will never be religious again, faith in individual salvation will have been extirpated, and all spiritual energies will be used for the construction of a totally earthly society.

If Marxism considers the Church as its number one enemy, for inverse reasons the Church has condemned Marxism as the embodiment of anti-Christian doctrines. The argument that both Christianity and Marxism want to promote the good of men is fallacious because at issue is precisely *what* constitutes the good of man. Therefore when we hear today with increasing frequency that although Marxists and Christians disagree on matters of doctrine they should nevertheless cooperate in practical matters, we must dismiss the argument as pure propaganda and, at best, as an unexamined concept, because (1) doctrine is not a gratuitous symbol, it defines the kind of attitude it favors; and (2) action is not blind, it is directed toward a certain goal, in direct line with objectives on which Communists and Christians most certainly disagree. This is the reason why Pius XI called communism "intrinsically perverse," and warned that even when Communists approach Catholics with the lure of communication, the latter should refuse any such cooperation.

Why can Communists tempt Catholics with common action if their respective doctrines are opposed? Communism is not a new line of thought that originated in Marx, but the contemporary expression of the exclusive belief in mankind's self-fulfilment in the secular city. Under various names communism has accompanied Christianity in history, and will accompany it for the remainder of history, offering to Christians the temptation of facilitating their earthly happiness and to the Church the temptation of dominating the world through a kind of short-cut. If the burden of spirituality and of spiritual loyalty to the *Civitas Dei* is removed, Communists of all times have argued, then the objectives of Christianity can materialize in short order, for all mankind will help with a unity of purpose. The stumbling block is that Christians cannot give up their belief in Christ's salvific action, nor their loyalty to His promise. Thus there are and there always will be Christians who listen to the Communist lure (while Christ did *not* listen to Satan's tempting words!) and who say: Let us give up faith, or at least, let us suspend faith in all that the Church teaches because this is not what Christ taught. If we follow Christ but not the Church (which is an institution with ambiguous goals), we will find that, suitably translated into modern terms, Christ was also a Socialist, exhorting us with his example to work for the poor, against the rich, and for the happiness of all men. This is how the Gospel became in the minds of young Catholics a social gospel, either definitively or for a certain historical period.

Does this mean that the Church should have no contact with Communists and with countries under a Communist regime? This would be an impossibility because the Church must make great sacrifices of all kinds in order to keep the lines of communications open with Catholics living in those countries. This is an extremely complicated and difficult task of which more will be said in this chapter. What is at once obvious, however, is that with Communists everything must be done on a *quid pro quo* basis, a method they understand because it conforms to their own practice of the "dialectical" method. Such negotiations have nothing to do with the dialogue: negotiations are moves on the diplomatic level, the dialogue is the acceptance of a Trojan horse among Christians. Thus there is no real dialogue going on except the kind that the *Osservatore Romano* denounced in these terms:

> A rather unique dialogue: on the one side, the Communists assert that never, for no reason whatever, will they give up or even moderate their principles. On the other side, the "Catholics" answer that we shall see, and we should not get discouraged. Thus to a consistent attitude a dangerous and ambiguous pragmatism tries to answer.[1]

The Catholics whom the Roman journal placed between quotation marks are, of course, Church-intellectuals, which explains their chimerical mentality and unrealistic expectations. In both Europe and the United States they claim to speak for the Church and for Catholics in general, but in reality they are spokesmen of ephemeral groups, for a moment in the limelight. In Europe, the Church-intellectuals have long been seduced by a false image of the working class, an image fabricated by nineteenth-century socialism. This image derives its characteristic traits from that of the "noble savage" whom long before Rousseau and other Romantics, the alleged inventors of the term, the priests around the suave Archbishop Fénelon had begun to idealize. The myth was further refined by the Abbé Lamennais in the 1830s, by Saint-Simon's disciple, Pierre Leroux, and by the ancestors of the Russian revolutionaries, Bielinski and Herzen. Lamennais, as we have seen, proposed a plan to the pope of an alliance between Rome and the proletariat. Leroux, whose ideas circulated through the novels of his lady friend, Georges Sand, propagandized a "religion for humanity," synthetizing existing teachings with those of Robespierre. The two Russians are reported by Dostoevsky as believing that if Christ returned suddenly to the earth, he would take the leadership of the Socialist movement. Dostoevsky adds that in the 1840s it was fash-

[1] March 3, 1965.

ionable to compare socialism, just aborn, to Christianity, and
even to consider it as an improvement upon the Christian religion.[2]

Assimilated to Robespierre in the middle of the last century, Christ is assimilated to Marx today, a hundred years later.
But a kind of evolution in terminology and approach, an evolution negative to Christianity, is noticeable. In 1848 and before
the language of revolutionaries was permeated by religious references, or at least, religious emotions. In the middle of the twentieth century the Church-intellectuals do not even try to break
out of the limits imposed by the Marxist universe of discourse.
This is the condition of dialogue with Marxists who are careful
not to make even vocabulary concessions.

In the Anglo-Saxon countries Marxism did not penetrate
into public life to the same extent as in continental Europe, or
at least it penetrated under various disguises and became diluted
with other, at times homegrown ideologies. The Church-intellectuals in the United States, England, or Canada did not,
therefore, insist right away on a dialogue with the Marxists—although that was the ultimate wish and logical end. They first
had to soften up their public, and before everything else their
own sturdy Catholic laymen, through a "democratically" conducted dialogue with so-called "out-groups": youth of various
persuasion, beatniks, homosexuals, etc. In basically puritanic
societies that Anglo-Saxon countries have remained, such an activity or program has had the features of a scandal, so that
Church-intellectuals could, at a cheap cost, bask in the sunshine
of progressivism, daring, and tolerance, all at once. Anglican
bishops enter into silly discussions with beat singers on the BBC,
they promote liberalized laws on crime and homosexuality, and
eagerly seek publicity as chief witnesses at court trials of novels
like *Lady Chatterley's Lover*. In the United States there can be
today no proposal quaint enough for the Church-intellectuals
not to espouse it right away, whether priests sit-in at cardinals'

---

[2] Joseph Frank, "Dostoievski et les socialistes," *Le Contrat Social*, January–February 1966, p. 13.

offices, syndicalization of priests, "handcuffing" police,[3] liberalization of abortion laws, and abolition of priests' celibacy.

These are stages along the road to dialogue with Marxism. In Europe this dialogue is an actual political danger since the Communist parties are never too far from power or at least shared power through Popular Fronts; in Anglo-Saxon countries the dialogue helps social and moral disintegration because Marxism is admired not so much for its ideological content (of which relatively little is known), let alone for its economic accomplishments (its failure is fairly well appreciated), as for its ability to corrode all social restraints in free societies. In Europe, the Catholic–Marxist dialogue helps, little or much, depending on the circumstances, to destroy the *political order*; in the United States it helps destroy the *social discipline* (civic virtues) on which stability and wellbeing rest.

It is time to examine the Church-intellectuals' motivation for dialogue with Marxism, and the mechanism of this dialogue. Historically, the first great and lasting experience of the Church was her long centuries in the catacombs, then sudden emergence to light, recognition, and power. This experience cannot be erased from the Church's memory, it influences other, later episodes in the relationship of Church and State. Briefly, during three hundred years Christianity had penetrated all classes of Roman society, first the slaves, then entire households with their women and children, finally the powerful themselves. Because of its peaceful nature, Christianity naturally takes this road, and not a frontal attack. It conquers through internal conversion, although it may look like subversion as viewed by the conquered State.

The belief of Church-intellectuals that the Church may now be standing before a new "Roman period" turned into firm conviction after 1945 and Soviet Russian penetration into the heart of Europe. Many of them had maintained for quite some time that the bourgeoisie is irrevocably degenerating and is los-

[3] Lead article in the *Catholic World*, February 1967.

ing confidence in itself. In Italy, writes Carlo Falconi,[4] Catholic intellectuals like Dossetti, Fanfani, La Pira believed that the "Communist steamroller" was going to flatten Europe first, then the United States; the objective of the Church should be "to conquer the conqueror," but not without first renovating herself in "silence, prayer, and sacrifice." The first experience, that of the catacombs, was to be repeated; to deserve success in the end, the Church was to withdraw her support from an undeserving, agonizing capitalistic world.

This analysis is half-Christian, half-Marxist, and also somewhat opportunistic because made in the shadow of Soviet guns looking down threateningly on Europe from Berlin, the Vistula, and the Adriatic. Thus the question arises: Have these Church-intellectuals been intent on saving the Church by camouflaging it, or, having lost their faith under the fire of Marxist critique, have they transferred their allegiance to Marxism which they hope ultimately to liberalize into a domesticated form of the secular city?

This seems to me the most important question that can be raised concerning this particular brand of dialogue, for the answer we give decides whether the dialogue has at least an element of genuineness or whether it is a sham, an act of shadow boxing, a match lost in advance to the opponent.

No clearcut answer can be given simply because in the present undisciplined state of the Church everybody says and does what he pleases, and even the dialoguers do not agree among themselves. I mentioned before that in Latin America the leftist clergy, believing the continent to be on the threshold of industrialization and of management-worker conflicts, wishes to be in the forefront of events by taking unilaterally and without studying all the factors of the situation the side of the workers, of socialist planning, and generally leftist policies. If this clergy's voice prevailed in Latin America during the next decades, the continent would hardly develop economically, and social conflicts would become possibly worse than in the past.

4 *Vu et entendu au Concile* (Monaco, Editions du Rocher, 1965).

In France, the now ex-Father Montuclard taught in the 1950s that Christianity had sinned so grievously against the poor in the past centuries that now when the poor (the proletariat) has finally found a worthy and efficient champion in the Communist party, charity would demand of the Church to step aside until the working class is economically liberated. Then Catholics may again start preaching the Gospel since well-fed workers might pay more attention to its message. Thus Montuclard and others developed one of the basic premises that the dialoguers, in advance agreement across the dividing line, are exploiting: faith is not another dimension, namely God's grace and the penetration of Christ in our soul, but is conditioned by social reality. In other (Marxist) words, faith is part of the superstructure, its contents and form change with changing economic conditions. Since, in Marxist theory, the classless Communist society will have absorbed the need for superstructure: literature, art, law, religion, and so on, there will be no faith, no belief in God, no Church.

Nobody denies that the Catholic interlocutors of the dialogue are men practising their faith as sincere Christians. But their influence on the faithful, and, when they are priests, on the whole of ecclesiastical life, is not derived from their inner conformity to Catholic duties but from their public writings and utterances. Can they be called good Catholics in this respect? Carlo Falconi, who is one of them, gives an eye-opening answer to his own question, "Can the progressives still call themselves Catholics?":

If we mean by Catholicism—and what else can we mean?—that which distinguishes this Christian community from other historical denominations, namely papal primacy and infallibility, the spirit of the Curia and of Canon Law, the spirit of scholasticism, and temporal choices in politics then there is no doubt: the genuine Catholics are behind the blind eye and convulsive gestures of Ottaviani. . . . The progressives who aspire to return to the Christianity of the first centuries, in the domain of ideology and of

structure, liturgy and discipline, are essentially Evangelists
. . . and they are destined to de-Catholicize the Church.[5]

Perhaps unwittingly, Falconi puts his finger on a very important point. Those whom he calls "progressives" have made a selection of what they accept and what they reject from Church doctrine and discipline. For good measure, he even calls them Evangelists, the name given to sixteen-century pre-Reformers and Reformers who usually ended up in Luther's or Calvin's camp. The natural thing would be then that these progressives should leave the Church since in their hearts and minds they are schismatic already. They have obviously decided to remain inside the Church in order eventually to "de-Catholicize" it. Whether they will succeed is a question we cannot answer. But can they really be genuine partners, representatives of the Church, in a dialogue with the Church's self-confessed enemies? The answer to this question needs no elaboration, but the issue becomes further clarified when we realize that these dialoguing Church-intellectuals prove their partisanship for Marxism by having the same enemies as the Marxists, namely their traditionalist fellow-Catholics.[6]

In the above-quoted passage, Falconi denounces the "temporal choices in politics" by those whom he derisively labels "Catholics," apparently a term of opprobrium. He means an anti-Marxist political choice. He conveniently forgets that Catholics are not only entitled to this choice as free in temporal matters, but are expressly encouraged by Pius XI's encyclical on communism and by various pronouncements of Pius X, Pius XII, and Paul VI. But Falconi implies even more: namely, that an anti-Marxist stance is a *political* choice, whereas a pro-

[5] *Op. cit.*, pp. 251–252. Note that "Evangelist" was the name of the sixteenth-century pre-Reformers, most of whom later joined Calvin in Geneva.

[6] Gilbert Mury, first-line philosopher of the French Communist Party, noted (in *La France Nouvelle*, March 31, 1965) that it is obvious at every new dialogue that Communists and progressive Catholics stand together, and that only a small band of conservative Catholics (Integrists) tries still to wreck their agreement. G. Mury has, since he wrote this article, transferred his allegiance to the Maoist faction of Communism.

Marxist stance is a *nonpolitical* choice,[7] he would perhaps even call it a naturally human, a naturally Christian choice.

Indeed, much of the dialoguers' eagerness to reach a formal agreement with Marxism has been conditioned by their hatred for non-leftist Catholics. While in communism they see a correct, even Christian inspiration, in traditional Catholicism they see only an obstacle to progress. In other words, they reproach traditional Catholics with not understanding and obstructing mankind's forward march and with slowing down the energizing process that this forward march could obtain from Communist–Catholic cooperation. This is how one can explain that a prominent French Church-intellectual, Father Andre Liege, could say this enormity: "The integrists [traditionalists] are the Church's worst enemies, more dangerous than the Communists."

All this was made clear many times and by various Church-intellectuals who treat the problem in a true Marxist spirit, the spirit of class struggle. This political overtone (or should we say, this political motivation?) gives the entire reformist, updating movement, even to certain aspects of the Council, a dubious coloration, as if reforms were in the interest of an ideological position rather than of the Church as a whole, and as if the object of the "progressives" were to dominate the Church, excluding their enemies therefrom. Father Yves Congar, whose great work, V*raie et fausse reforme dans l'Eglise,* did so much to accelerate the calling together of the Council, and who assured his readers that "there is nothing revolutionary in the present [1950] reform movement, either in France or elsewhere" (p. 570.), could not end his book without launching an unwarranted attack on those whom he calls "conservatives." Fifteen years before Falconi he made the essentially Marxist point that conservatism ("integrism") is tied to political attitudes, whereas the other position to which he gives no name since he views it as a natural position, is "open to the modern world, without any political option." Integrism, he writes, is tied to "definite ob-

[7] Needless to say, this is exactly the Marxist thesis: *politics* is practiced by the oppressors of the proletariat; the proletarian State where ownership is collective, has suppressed the political principle. Marx *dixit!*

jects" (materialism?); the other position is "simply an attitude of the mind." And he adds: "Integrism is characterized by a distrust of human beings" (*op. cit.* pp. 611 and 617).

Some seven years later the same aggressiveness appears in an article by Georges Hourdin, another prominent Church-intellectual, a layman. The tone is obsessively divisive, the content frankly Marxist. The integrists, Hourdin writes, reject the modern world and try to put a brake on its development. They want to restore the old economic structure and colonialism. The progressives, on the contrary, condemn the modern world for the opposite reason: that it has stopped at the Capitalist phase. They hope that evolution will bring with it socialization and a morally better world in whose construction the Church will also take an important part. This is why the (Catholic) progressives are willing to enter the struggle against capitalism on the side of the Communists who speak in the name of the popular masses. And Hourdin adds, in agreement with Montuclard: "The preaching of the Gospel to peasants and workers will only be possible after they have acquired a higher standard of living." [8]

This article appeared in June 1957, hardly seven months after the Hungarian popular insurrection which proved beyond any possible doubt that communism does not create a higher standard of living for "peasants and workers," and that, in fact, it robs all classes of society, except the "new class" of privileged party leaders, of even a modest level of wellbeing and security. But again: I quoted this text not to prove the hopeless incompetence of M. Hourdin in matters of economic policy, but to illustrate his uncritical partisanship for the Communist cause and his equally uncritical acceptance of world-Communist slogans. If he typifies the dialoguing Catholics, and according to my observation, he does, then how seriously can we take the dialogue, and how can we not suspect that he is part of a fifth column within the Church?

A brief examination of these dialogues in the concrete will give us the answer. In the first place, they usually are organized in non-Communist countries because Communist governments

[8] *Le Monde*, June 6, 1957.

prefer not to have either communism or religion openly discussed within their borders. This is at first sight surprising since
the discourses expected of non-Communist participants would
not be hostile to the regime, anyway. The latter could even display the support, be it indirect, it receives from men reputedly
hostile to communism, such as a priest or a lay Catholic. Yet,
Communist regimes prefer to miss such opportunities rather
than suggest to their own restless populations that free discussion on these matters is still possible.

In the second place, these dialogues provide the Communists with invaluable propaganda opportunities. One such opportunity is to create and spread the reputation of Communist
intellectuals as serious scholars seeking the truth; another opportunity is subtly to operate a selection in the Catholic camp:
those Catholics who are willing to enter the dialogue are the
better, the more courageous, the more objective people, while
those who refuse the dialogue become, by definition, reactionary, inadequate as scholars, prejudiced as men.

In the third place, the Catholic dialoguers are in advance
convinced at least of the acceptability of Communist arguments and try to show that in a number of respects the two
positions coincide. This, on the other hand, is not acknowledged
by the Communist interlocutors unless they have succeeded in
getting their opponents nearer to their own position, without
themselves moving away from it.

My first two points indicate the setting and the personnel
of the dialogue; it is easy to see that Communists can never lose
in this game. But it is the third point that is crucial from their
point of view, and they never cease to exploit fully their built-in
advantages. Crudely put: the Catholic participants arrive with
an inferiority feeling since for reasons discussed before they are
ideologically at least half-convinced of the validity of the opponent's arguments or of the dynamism of his power-drive. The
Communists, on the other hand, arrive as the sure victors: since
it is accepted as a premise that the world is increasingly secularized, the Catholics fight a timid rear-guard action, the Communists represent the future. Any minor concession they might

make only shows their generosity.[9] Their victories are easily won since they are true believers in their cause and elite minds of their party; neither could be affirmed of their Catholic opponents. Consequently, the Catholic thesis on such occasions[10] is presented by Church-intellectuals only remotely in agreement with Catholic doctrine and Catholic position. The "updating" seems not only to permit any kind of extravagance *intra muros,* but also authorizes various personal theories to represent at these meetings the Church's voice. At any rate, they are eagerly taken as authoritative by the Communists and by the press reporting the events. Thus at Chiemsee (May 1966) Karl Rahner proposed a version of his negative theology, insisting that God is unknowable. He declared that from a Christian point of view this impossibility to know God makes many kinds of humanisms acceptable, provided they do not claim to be absolute. Since, he added, Marxism is not an absolute humanism, there is no obstacle to the dialogue!

This statement proves admirably the point I made earlier: the Church-dialoguer accepts in advance a weak position, then goes on to offer a platform to his opponent which is imaginary but which would authorize the so-much-desired dialogue. In other words, the Church-intellectuals enter the debate with a mixture of bad faith, masochism, and illusion. Their Marxist opponents do not suffer from these ills. Their tactical position is that the dialogue is possible if both sides "get rid of their extremists": the Catholics of Pius XII, conservatism, and the tradition, the Communists of the "remnants of the Stalin era." They offer, in other words, the repudiation of a regime which did not affect Marxism as a doctrine, in exchange for Catholic repudiation of the essence of Christianity. An excellent move

[9] Fr. Edward Duff, S.J., participant at a World Conference on Church and Society organized by the World Council of Churches in Geneva (July 1966), remarked that under violent attack "the humility and patience, sometimes bordering on masochism, of the westerners, especially the Americans, under such attacks was admirable." (*America,* August 27, 1966).

[10] Outstanding among these are the *Semaine des Intellectuels Catholiques,* the *Semaine de la Pensée Marxiste,* the Chiemsee (Bavaria) colloquium, the Paulus Gesellschaft (Austria), etc.

since it would force the Church into a vague Protestant attitude
—indeed Rahner's attitude mentioned above!

The Communists, on the other hand, make no doctrinal
concessions. In his book, *From Anathema To Dialogue*, Roger
Garaudy, chief philosopher of the French Communist party,
continues to stand by his Marxist materialism and reasserts his
belief that religions will die out when communism materializes.
At the most, he admits (in an article for the far-leftist Catholic
Témoignage Chrétien, March 1965) that in its victorious march
Marxism may want to assimilate the "human substance" of
Christianity. But he adds that the Christians themselves ought
to rejoice at this since otherwise their religion would remain a
"disincarnated spiritual system."

This position is also Father Teilhard de Chardin's who believed that today's Christianity will yield to a "meta-Christian-
ity" in which the two evolutionary drives: upward (*en haut*)
and forward (*en avant*) will merge. The Communists and their
Catholic partisans interpret Teilhard's "forward" as best expressed in Marxism. No wonder that Garaudy at Chiemsee had
high praise for Teilhard whose "passion for the universe," he
said, represents the greatest challenge for a nonbeliever.

The Catholic dialoguers, in turn, eagerly welcome these
sentimental (never doctrinal!) crumbs thrown to them. They
rush to heap insults on fellow-Catholics of a different conviction, claim the possibility of doctrinal integration with Marxism,[11] show childish impatience for joint action with the Communists, and accept even a materialistic interpretation of history
and morals. One wonders what remains to be dialogued about
when a Roger Garaudy may sum up, after a week's discussions
with Catholic priests:

> When a Fr. Dubarle admits the value of scientific ma-
> terialism . . . when Fr. Jolif brings to the surface those
> values which are immanent in the materialistic conception

[11] The Catholic D. Zolo in *Il dialogo alla prova* ("The dialogue put to
the test") made up of essays by Italian Communists and Catholics, sees
"the possibility of a doctrinal integration of some aspects of Marxist humanism with aspects of the Christian conception of man." (Florence, 1964).

of ethics . . . when both argue that Catholics and Communists may cooperate in the elaboration of a common humanism . . . then a new step forward has been made.[12]

I said above that the meeting place of Catholic–Communist dialogue is usually on non-Communist-controlled territory. But it is interesting to inquire into Communist governments' policies with regard to the Catholic religion and Church. After all, these policies ought to be affected by the dialogue, particularly since the Communists' religious policies in the entire Soviet orbit are rather monolithic: if Garaudy and his comrades are authorized to enter the dialogue with members of the Church, this new attitude must mean a tactical modification in Communist governmental policies. Only if these policies showed some changes in the direction of more freedom granted to the Church, could we say that the dialogue is a sign of sincere Communist desire to reach a settlement.

The Communists have a well-defined policy of dealing with the Church, following the strategy summed up by Lenin himself: "To finish off religion, it is much more important to introduce the class struggle within the Church than to attack directly religion itself." What we see today in this respect is never a basic change of this theme, only variations thereon. In Poland, China, Cuba, and elsewhere the policy is outlined and applied in several stages: enrollment of Catholics in popular movements aimed at dissociating them from Rome; then many of them, becoming aware of what is planned, show resistance. The next step is to try and punish the leaders of the resistance as enemies of the regime. Those who dare manifest no disagreement with these procedures are enrolled in a "patriotic" national Church, under a hierarchy enjoying the Communist party's confidence. This "hierarchy," recruited through intimidation or bribe, exists and has power by the permission of its bosses. Thus the members of the hierarchy are not only obedient executors of Communist policy inside their mock Church, they are also spies of the Communist government, obliged to report whoever in this "national

[12] *L'Humanité*, January 27, 1965.

Church" would follow a more independent line. The delegation of the Hungarian bishops to the Council was, for example, under permanent surveillance by a few priests, also members of the delegation. The pattern is the same as in Communist embassies all over the world where the driver or the gardener may be a hierarchic superior of the ambassador himself in the Communist party apparatus, and entrusted with the duty of controlling the latter's actions.

The biggest such false Church in existence is in Poland. Strictly speaking, it is not a Church but a movement, called *Pax*, headed by a known secret police stooge, Boleslav Piasecki. An ex-Nazi, he was recruited after the war by Soviet NKVD General Ivan Serov who promised him freedom from execution in exchange for his help in undermining Poland's Church, an unshakable obstacle in the country's communization. The Pax movement has had two functions: the weakening of the Polish Church through the techniques I outlined above, and the subversion of French Catholics with whom the Poles have always had a particularly close and trusting relationship. The overall plan was to show the French Church-intellectuals, the closest to Marxism and the most influential in Christendom, that Christianity is compatible with communism and that the future of religion depends anyway on its good behavior under Communist regimes. If we remember that Church-intellectuals in the West are by and large convinced of ultimate Communist victory, then it becomes clear why they welcomed so eagerly the Pax movement which showed them the pattern of collaboration. Zenon Kliszko, vice-president of the Polish parliament and personal emissary of Party-Secretary Gomulka to the Council, declared in Rome that the overall objective of the Party remains the systematic repression of clericalism and the carrying out of a complete laicization. He added at a press conference that the Church must draw her own conclusions from Polish socialist reality which will not become less intransigent with the passing of years.

When the Church-intellectuals were duly impressed by this brutal talk, Gomulka dispatched Piasecki to Rome who declared that the only alternative left to Polish Catholics was between enrollment in Pax and complete disappearance. This shows how well the Communists know the Church-intellectuals and their psychology: they offer them the dialogue, then brutally tell them that they have no other choice than to accept what is offered. The Church-intellectuals are even provided with an excuse: if they refuse, Catholicism will cease to exist. The Church-intellectual will have a good conscience after such a treatment: after all, he only yielded in order to save his fellow Catholics.

More than that: he is thus given a chance to "build socialism." With an irrevocable and uncritical hatred of capitalism, middle classes, and generally the Western political-social structure, the Church-intellectual aspires at least at a vicarious role in the construction of the socialist state. It may be that he hopes for more freedom for his Church after a new "Roman period" is over. Meanwhile, however, his stand is indistinguishable from that of the Socialists', and indeed, Communists'. George Ronay, a Hungarian Catholic participant at the *Semaine des intellectuels catholiques* (March 1965) summed up in these words what he considers the only realistic attitude of Catholics living in a Marxist state: "We, believers, must show the way to God by proving ourselves as the most efficient builders of socialism." [13]

Even if we were to admit the validity of the thesis that all the Church can do facing the Communist Juggernaut is to go underground and wait for better times, we would find that these Church-intellectuals' actions do not conform to this thesis. True, the Christians under the Roman Empire were constructive citizens and good soldiers. Their civic virtues were grudgingly recognized, if not officially by the State, at least by their fellow citizens in daily contact. But their social usefulness was not put into the service of the future secular state founded on the principle of crushing their hopes, nor did they surrender their religious loyalty to the gods of the existing pagan state. The comparison with today's situation is based on a fundamen-

[13] *Témoignage Chrétien,* March 18, 1965.

tal error in outlook; Mr. Ronay and his Western Church-intellectual colleagues invite Catholics to accept the Marxist state *together with* its gods, not merely to act like loyal citizens of the temporal state.

The Catholic–Marxist dialogue is shot through with contra-dictions, bad faith, mental reservations. On the one hand, a pro-Marxist position of the Catholic side, on the other an un-abashed "triumphalism" of the Communist side. Both agree in advance that Christianity is an egoistic religion because it con-cerns itself with individual salvation. Then a short step, assert-ing that capitalism, also a selfish view of the world, is inspired by the Christian spirit: to destroy capitalism, Christianity must first be transformed. Both sides also agree that socialism means con-cern for people, not only economic concern but for their dignity as well. Thus the transformation of Christianity must proceed along Socialist lines. The Church-intellectual has the choice of either becoming a secular Socialist (in which case he loses his usefulness for the Communists as a partner in dialogue), or an enthusiastic promoter of socialism inside the Church and inside societies still influenced by the Church. The Marxists need him in this second role.

All this becomes even more obvious when we examine the projection of the dialogue-gatherings. Communists and the Church-intellectuals adopt the same position with regard to the tasks they wish to assume in common and the task they recom-mend to the Church. In the *West* they advertise the absolute necessity for the Church to involve itself in the activities of building a more "human" society. The Church, they say, must assume, after centuries of aloofness, its role as leaven of the community and of history, must immerse itself in the battle for a better world, even if this means alienating certain groups and classes labeled "conservative." For this purpose, the Church should accept that Catholics, priests and laymen, march side by side with other progressive groups, even adopt their violent or revolutionary methods.

The whole approach changes when the Church-intellectuals, again in agreement with the Communists, advise the Church about the best behavior in the *East,* in Communist countries. There the assignment given to the Church is strict spirituality and noninterference with the temporal domain which is the exclusive responsibility of the regime. It is recalled that the Church was founded for the care of the souls; it is pointed out that the Church can blame only herself if she takes the liberty of telling the State what it should do. This would be interpreted as the "politization" of the Church.

The conclusion is clear: the Church is encouraged to subvert western societies, but is told to withdraw from the affairs of the community when communism takes over. Nobody, least of all the Church, should interfere with the construction of socialism which needs no other guide than the Communist party. Let us bear in mind that this advice appears every day in Catholic newspapers of the progressive variety, not only in the subservient press of the East, but also in the liberal Catholic press of the West. It helps the Communist regimes solve their problem of first neutralizing, then abolishing religion. It promotes their objective of dominating the ecclesiastical apparatus within their borders. It puts the seal of approval on their policy never to allow religion to be propagated or even defended against the attacks of its enemies, indeed the attacks launched or sponsored by Party and State. Finally, it helps weakening religion as a possible focus of discontent whose growth would threaten total Communist power over people's lives.

This aid to abolish the Church and religion, to persecute Christians, jail their priests and bishops, close their schools and seminaries, lock them out of jobs—this aid is offered freely and enthusiastically by the Church-intellectuals through their "dialogue." If the Church survives Communist persecution, it will be thanks to its fearless spirit, its martyrs, its unshakable faith. As the example of Poland shows, the triumph of faith is achieved not through intellectuals lying low while the storm of persecution passes over them, but through the faith and confidence of the ordinary Catholics who form one body and soul with their militant hierarchy.

VII

IDEOLOGUES
IN THE CHURCH

Two things ought to be clear from the foregoing chapters: the first is that the Church today faces a crisis comparable only to the times when Arianism all but conquered it from within; the second is that the "dialogue" is hardly designed to bring about the union of Christian churches and fraternity with other religions, but that it is a camouflaged ideology working also within the Church and directed at her secularization.

I mention Arianism and not the sixteenth century Reformation as a time of great tribulation because the Church is at times better, at other times less well prepared to resist and overcome onslaughts against her. The long persecution from which she had just emerged under Emperor Constantine was perhaps one reason why the Church was unaccustomed to the light of day and the subtleties of politics. It is true that in Athanasius the Church was immensely fortunate to find an intrepid champion, but we can measure the gravity of the situation by the fact that even the Pope Liberius, proved at one time too weak to stand up to the coalition forces of Empire and bishops.

Quite different was the case in the sixteenth century when the Church had excellent theologians and, above all, a succession of strong popes. The Council of Trent, called together only a generation after the first explosion of protest, accomplished a brilliant doctrinal work and firmly restored discipline. The significance of this Council was that the Church as a healthy body reacted promptly to the danger, and was able to develop ways of neutralizing the poison injected in her body.

Today's Church, on the other hand, reflects the confusion characterizing the world. One look at the philosophies which are popular and the applications to which they are put, suffices for us to agree with Georges Bernanos' statement that modern civilization is a conspiracy against man. Man as he lives in a state of equilibrium, guided by common sense in most of his undertakings, able to absorb the shocks of existence because he is protected, not assailed, by institutions and the wielders of public influence. The crisis that besets the Church should be seen on both the supernatural and the natural level. The two cannot be dissociated because, as human beings, we live on both levels and they intermingle within us. It is a fashionable error to pretend that all we are facing now is a *cultural crisis*, not a crisis of the faith. And that all the Church ought to do is to adjust and update her traditional religious expressions to the needs of modern culture, the modern urban citizen, the industrial worker, the democratic procedures. But *man* remains the same under all the forms that culture imposes on him; true, he should and does adjust to the new and ever-changing civilizational forms, but if that is all he does and is advised to do, then he ends up confused and uprooted since under the fleeting phenomenon of change no substratum, no stability remains to steady him. In spite of today's fashionable preaching to adjust to a changing world and to change itself, nobody yet managed to live in the *flux*, internalize change, make of change a way of life. Least of all the preachers of the flux who, instead of learning and changing, settle comfortably and do their best to make their preferred "change" permanent.

All the while, *man,* for whose salvation Jesus Christ came, is assailed not only in his "cultural patterns" but also in his faith. For again, the two cannot be separated: what we do in life follows from what we are, what we believe to be true or false, good or bad. And conversely these convictions are strengthened or weakened in us according to the prevailing public philosophy, the leaders we follow, the schools we attend, the books we read, the advice we receive. The objective observer will not fail to note that this public philosophy today has turned against the human beings that we are: power has taken the place of love, self-expression that of beauty, propaganda and the "image" that of truth. Most things with which we are confronted are ugly, distorted, cynical, inarticulate, amounting not to a critical but a caricatural version of reality. The human being himself is "reduced" to the level of rats' behavior in the maze, the mother's love to the chemistry of hormones, simple belief to naïve acceptance of a myth. Parents are told that they endanger the healthy development of their children, and children are told that it is psychologically justified to hate their parents. Women were told recently in a symposium of blue stockings that "birth control surely represents the assertion of woman's rights to modify her biological nature as such in order to release her other intellectual and cultural potential." [1]

It is not my intention to exhaust here the subject of cultural decay in today's world, only to show that through a natural osmosis the "cultural crisis" and the religious crisis have intermingled the poison which is essentially the same in both. The Catholic suffers today from the same ills *qua* Catholic in the Church as he does as citizen, consumer, or simply member of the anonymous public, outside the Church. This in itself ought to settle the argument of a supposedly needed adaptation of Catholics to the world, since basically both the Church and the world are in need not of mutual adaptation, but of adaptation to the norms of truth and true faith. But, of the two, the Church is by far the guiltier since it was appointed to teach the

[1] "The Woman Intellectual and the Church," *Commonweal,* January 27, 1967.

world, not to join it, particularly when it is confused; to cure it particularly when it is sick.

The type of civilization Bernanos denounced has now penetrated into the Church, bringing with it its typical taste for ugliness, false propaganda, adoration of efficiency, opportunism, and derision of everything noble and innocent. I repeat that this civilization, defective in its own right, becomes particularly repulsive when adopted by the Church. For the Church lends it the authority it cannot completely possess in the world, and smuggles it into the lives of the faithful who least expect it from such trusted quarters. *Mutatis mutandis,* the same thing takes place in the religious life of Catholics as in the function of parents as the rightful first educators of their children. Unsuspecting, today's parents send their children to school and expect that the school will cooperate with the moral duties entrusted to it by God through natural law. Instead, in all too many cases, teachers, psychologists, and administrators conspire to demolish the child's reverential heart for God, parent, the moral law, and the norms on which civilized life rests.

Similarly in the Church today. Emboldened by the Vatican Council, the "new breed" priests, a very small minority but, as explained before, with a voice amplified by the secularistic, anti-spiritual media, impose new forms of liturgy, doctrine, and personal interpretation of discipline, in other words, new "cultural" forms behind which, however, the new faith is unmistakable. God has entrusted His flock to these priests, expecting the latter to cooperate with Him. Instead of which this arrogant new-breed clergy experiments with new forms but in reality it pushes around concrete men and women over whom it uses a usurped authority. Usurped, because used to ends contrary to the original assignment.

On whom does final responsibility rest? On the bishops and other prelates whose behavior today recalls not the sixteenth century but the fourth, the age of Arian heresy. They display the same ambiguity as in Arius' time: *hardness* toward the faithful whose traditional reverence is intact and who, therefore, remain obedient to faith and *through* faith to authority; *slavishness* toward the powers of the day, mostly the media of communication, ever-ready to attack, deride, criticize the "unprogressive"; and *hesitance*, if not outright cowardice before the new-breed priest who is aggressive and arrogant, and whose alliance with the powers of the day these bishops and monsignors know well but dare not denounce.

This is, in plain words, the situation in today's Church, a situation that it is not enough to analyze sociologically or psychologically since it happens not in a political party, business enterprise, club or classroom, but in the Church. Therefore the responsibilities are infinitely heavier and the shepherds infinitely guiltier. Because, as Evelyn Waugh noted writing about the Council, "a Catholic believes that whatever is enacted at the Council will ultimately affect the entire human race." [2]

Since history is hung up, so to speak, on the peg of divine providence, the Church is never allowed to become corrupted in all its parts at once. While empires and nations disappear without a trace, the Church's history shows a continuous miracle insofar as it is saved by a strong papacy, a newly inspired religious order, the works of a saint, or indeed by the ordinary laity. It is of the latter that Evelyn Waugh wrote with true insight and modesty (since he included himself in their rank): "In every age we have formed the main body of the 'faithful' and we believe that it was for us, as much as for the saints and for the notorious sinners, that the Church was founded." [3] Today it befalls the laity to save the Church in her embarrassment and scandal. The Vatican Council wisely decided, perhaps more wisely than the bishops knew, to give a greater voice to the laity in the Church's affairs, in fact to adjoin them to Church activity at every level. The wisdom of the move can be seen as the desire of an equilibrium at a time when another element of the Church, the intellectuals, is so dangerously playing with sacred things. To be sure, this equilibrium will not be evident for some time: just as totalitarian parties define arbitrarily whom they consider builders of their regime and whom enemies of the peo-

[2] *National Review*, December 1962.
[3] Idem.

ple, so the Church-intellectuals, with the prelates who unthinkingly join them sensing their power, select that segment of the laity which is ready to obey, echo the slogans, emit the expected noises. The others, the majority, are insulted, treated with contempt, dismissed as backward and primitive. Yet things will become clear, gradually, with painful slowness.

At first, there was stunned acceptance: in the United States where special circumstances prevail, the laity hardly ever expressed opinions contrary to the clergy, and never developed the anticlericalism so essential for the above-mentioned equilibrium. Thus when the Church-intellectuals grew to the point of constituting a class and even penetrated the ranks of the clergy, any sign of rebellion against the new breed was paralyzed. The Church-intellectuals who have so regularly mocked the monolithism of American Church and sighed with envy before the freedom and anarchism of Protestants and Jews allegedly more in line with the American pattern of pluralism and democracy, now are intolerantly severe with those who contradict them from the ranks, and want to enforce an absolute uniformity. "I find most reprehensible," writes Mr. Dan Herr, "that . . . the new breed clergy and lay leaders . . . hold the pious laity in contempt. . . . It is ironic that these are the same people who in the past claimed to exalt the role of the laity." [4] Alas, this is how the most accomplished persecutors are recruited from among the persecuted!

In Europe the point of departure was different: there the laity learned through repeated historical lessons that power must be limited, including that of the Church hierarchy. Anticlericalism among Catholics has been a long tradition, taken as a matter of fact. The Church-intellectuals appeared as champions of the great reconciliation between the Church and the "masses" (Lamennais' "alliance of Pope and proletariat"), and managed to seduce the bishops with the prospect of power through a common front with the "working class." There was hardly any question of the workers in this transaction, and nobody really cared to consult them. The workers were represented in the

[4] *Overview*, February 1, 1967.

"dialogue" by the intellectuals themselves, Catholic and other. The goal was prestige for the Church-intellectuals, and prestige in a Church generally uninformed about the world meant power, namely the power to transform the Church.

The whole question, then, whether in the United States or in Europe, can be reduced to this: How to strengthen the Catholic layman against the Church-intellectuals so that the hierarchy may also regain her former authority over this rebellious class.

The existence of the conflict, opposing Rome and the national Churches, the Church-intellectuals and the laymen, conservative and progressive bishops, etc., can no longer be denied. It is not necessary to call it class war, although as we have seen it in the previous chapter, it has similar features and might be transformed into one. In more Christian terms, the conflict arises from the fact that the Church-intellectuals have by and large accepted the post-Christian era as a reality, even as a desirable reality, and have subscribed to the analysis of a Feuerbach, a Comte, a Marx, a Nietzsche, leading to the abolition of Christianity. There is, as it can be ascertained, a variety of inspirations, and Marx's is only one among several. But they all agree that man is now emancipated from belief in God, that God was a projection of mankind's aspirations and potentialities, and that a thus liberated mankind's natural vocation is to create paradise on earth.

It is, however, not the people supposedly called to build this paradise, but the intellectuals interpreting the signs of its nearness who spin endless theories about the ultimate meaning and goal of the industrial society. Feuerbach, urged by his students to put his theories to test and engage in direct action, replied: "We are not yet advanced enough to pass from theory to its application." [5] Today, "direct action" by professors, students, intellectuals—and priests—is an everyday occurrence, and the sense of power experienced by them moves them in the direction of proclaiming man's self-sufficiency. As *modern men,*

---

[5] Quoted by Henri de Lubac, S.J., *Le Drame de l'humanisme athée* (Paris, Editions Spes., 1944), p. 48.

they deny the eternal; as *post-Christian men*, they deny the relevance of God. Kierkegaard wrote of their nineteenth-century ancestors that they hold that faith is a shelter for weak minds and that the task of intellectuals is "to go further than" the Christianity of the Apostles. The Dane, whose life was spent in combating the "philosophers, professors, and intellectuals," added what amounts to both observation and prophecy: in their naïve and self-satisfied pedantism these men discuss "God who is no more," build all kinds of abstract systems on this supposition, but carefully avoid any passionate commitment to faith. But how can one speak of God, Kierkegaard asked (in the *Post-Scriptum*), with only a cold mental approach?

The cleavage that Kierkegaard observed among Protestants only, has grown since and is now strikingly evident, although still not quite believed yet, among Catholics also. I mean the cleavage between Church-intellectuals and laymen. Secular intellectuals do not speak of laymen but of "masses," that is an undifferentiated aggregate of people who think, act, and become politically important as a mass. Yet, such a mass does not exist *in concreto*, they only have an existence as instruments of class struggle, as a battering ram storming some citadel which resists the revolution. But the essence of Christianity makes it impossible to us to use the term "masses" in reference to laity. Not masses but individuals, human persons fill the Churches on Sundays, go to the sacraments, listen to sermons. Since the Church is a structured community, these faithful obey the clergy in matters where the latter possesses authority, and listen to the hierarchy and the pope in what they declare on matters of faith and morals. They never constitute a mass and never can be treated as such. Yet, the Church-intellectuals have now learned to manipulate the notion of mass inside the Church as it is done outside, in the modern, technical-industrial mass society. They seem also to have taken out entire pages from the book of Marxism by trying to operate among the majority of laymen through a minority supposedly speaking for all, but in reality echoing only the intellectuals. We are at a stage when it may be said without exaggeration that as Marx regarded the State, so they regard the Church: the first preached the withering away of the State, the intellectuals expect the withering away of the Church.

At the bottom of all the affirmations that man has come of age is the demand addressed to the Christian to become a *man*, that is more than a Christian. This "coming of age," as various writers diagnose and describe it, is in reality an invitation to accept as definitive in history the urban way of life with all its comforts, automation, electronics, as well as the sociological and political concomitants that are supposed to follow from so much technical sophistication. Just as the world is now open to unforeseen new discoveries and cosmic adventures, the Church must similarly open itself so as to accompany her members who have now reached adulthood. For the Church to be in the world, to contribute to the world, the last thing to do would be to continue enjoining a particular set of dogmas, articles of faith, and rigid attitudes. On the contrary, everything must be made flexible, yielding, confident in man's goodness and purposefulness guided by intelligence.[6] The change, the flux demands that the Church cease believing in essences, archetypes, models of the past to imitate and follow. Using the language of atheistic existentialism, Catholic intellectuals now say that free engagement in particular historical situations make it imperative that we remain open to the future. How could we then consider as model the saints, why should we read *The Imitation of Christ?* Sister Aloysius, in the already-mentioned "women's symposium," renews the Sophist Protagoras' main theme when she insists that "what is normative is not the natural but the personal." [7] In another attack on the Church's fidelity to essences and the permanence of truth, Professor Leslie Dewart argues (in his book, *The Future of Belief*) that the content of divine revelation is

[6] Let us note here that what the Church-intellectuals consider as revolutionary innovations in the Church and for which they proudly take credit, is, in the average, a generation behind the "world." In primary schools the Church in America is now introducing the theory and practice of permissiveness, rejected now even by the Deweyite citadel, the Teachers College of Columbia University.

[7] *Commonweal*, January 27, 1967, p. 450.

not known as communicated to us by Christ and fixed forever, but as an always renewed conceptualization of this message in the Church which responds to it according to the given sociohistorical milieu. The Church's response to revelation unravels in history, we therefore know only the response of our own time and should not try to preserve past responses, past forms of conceptualization.

These attacks against the metaphysics on which Christian philosophy rests are launched in the name of evolutionism, sophistry, phenomenology, and existentialism. Nothing new is expressed when Christianity and the Church are chosen as subjects. When, on the other hand, we would expect positive and original statements from the Church-intellectuals, we are treated to a repetition of fashionable platitudes. One would imagine, for example, that Professor Dewart has something worthwhile to say about a reconceptualization of revelation in our time. But since his real motivation is to show that Christians should melt into the contemporary milieu (for this purpose he has jettisoned the entire Greek philosophy) and that they should "dialogue" with Marxists and atheists who are, in his view, the real representatives of the milieu, he merely states that if Christianity became a revolutionary movement, then Marxists and atheists would not persevere in their opposition. Then atheists and Christians would cooperate in curing the ills of society.

It is noteworthy that all these Church-intellectuals are so completely sterile and unoriginal that their position is indistinguishable from that of secular sloganeers. This is to be expected since the Church-intellectual, having made his choice, must accept the prevailing slogans of the secular city. The world cannot wait until Omega Point becomes visible around the corner, but demands that the Church-intellectual translate his Christian eschatology into contemporary language, today the language of socialism and radical humanism. Thus the logic of absorption in the world, the eagerness with which priests stress the autonomy of worldly values, the almost complete absence of spirituality in their sermons, make these ecclesiastic and lay intellectuals indistinguishable from their secularistic colleagues. The urge to be worldly is hardly disguised in this passage of an editorial in *America* (December 3, 1966):

> The Pope's renewed mandate to the Society of Jesus to meet the grave challenge of radical secularism in the form of atheism is intelligible only to the degree to which Jesuits are free to share the basic insights and humanistic yearnings that pervade our age. To combat atheism today is a baroque or hidalgoist style would be both ridiculous and tragic.

This is of course the language of Tartuffe. To cure the sick, the physician must show compassion, but does not have to become sick himself. When Pope Paul, in speaking to the Jesuits, used the expression "sinister conspiracy" to describe what a substantial segment of the Order was engaging in, he was not in need of a lesson from *America* magazine concerning the Society, its strategy and loyalty.

The Tartuffian ambiguous approach pervades, for example, Karl Rahner's approval of the increasing role of the secular State in the affairs of men when, at the same time, he calmly recommends an increasingly modest role for the institutional Church in the spiritual life of the faithful. This same contradiction is manifest in the writings of all "new breed" intellectuals, starting with Fr. Teilhard de Chardin himself. They all greet the coming age of modern man and eulogize the latter's newly won freedom. Yet, on the next page they acquiesce that this freedom should be taken away and entrusted to the State or to the World State. They emancipate mankind from the spiritual sphere but subordinate it to the secular. A secular sphere which, precisely because it is left without competition, can only become totalitarian. Typically illogical is Rahner:

> The vast range of possibilities now opening out as a field of historical human decisions calls for an active entity capable of availing itself of those possibilities. . . . Such an entity is positively forced into existence. . . . It can only be the

State or the community of peoples organized at a planetary
level.[8]

This is obviously not an oversight on the part of a man
known to have a keen mind; it is an ideological position, conso-
nant with the fashionable secularistic creed. Adjustment to
change is loudly recommended by those holding this creed, but
they conveniently arrest change when their own ideological
hopes are satisfied. The only fixity the Church-intellectual condemns is that of the Church, or rather, he condemns the
Church for being an institution at all. The Protestant thesis
which later became secular dogma is alltooclearly visible under
the Roman collar: when everything is in flux and the Church
too is dissolved, the only stable point that may remain is the
subjective *self* as source of inspiration, judgment, and action.
With not much more crudeness and lack of logic than Rahner's,
the ladies of the *Commonweal* symposium did indeed reach this
conclusion. One of them, Sister Aloysius, declared that she welcomed the end of "Christendom" (her own quotation marks)
and the de-tribalization of Christians because such an identity
crisis happens naturally when people come of age. Another lady
then expressed the group's consensus that a "real free church
style would operate beyond denominational categories," would
have "no interest in traditional institutions at all, but rather
would celebrate around a community of concern." The implication is that the Church is *not* a community of concern, but a
backward, pompous, and useless institution, as indeed the dis-
cussants never tired repeating.

Enough has been said in this and other chapters about the
Church-intellectuals and their use of the "dialogue" for the
demoralization and secularization of the Church. In each of the
dialogue-attempts we found, first, their attitude of uncritical acceptance of the interlocutor's position, provided it was anti-
Catholic and radical. Secondly, we found a ruthless attack on
the spiritual in the name of the secular, since dialogue is con-

[8] *The Christian Commitment*, p. 13.

ducted not with the entire range of interlocutors, but only with the worldliest and shallowest among Protestants, Jews, atheists, —and Catholics. And thirdly, we found that the dialogue serves only as a disguise for bringing about the post-Christian age and the secular city.

The frightening thing in all this is not so much the ideology of the dialogue, the shallow content, the orientation toward a divinized mankind and the secular city. These are, as I stated at the beginning of this study, new versions of very old temptations, errors, heresies. In a way they fortify the Church, oblige her to take stock, feel her vitality, gather the faithful around her. Much more terrifying is the wreckage that the Church-intellectuals and ideologues visit upon the Church and its members: a destruction from which some ruins always remain. The Church is not an ordinary group of human beings with a history such as a nation or a movement have. An earthly community does not live in the dimension of eternity, it has a purely earthly end; if part of the community must sacrifice itself for the good of the whole, it is an acceptable sacrifice. But the Church has no objective in history other than leading her members to salvation; she cannot, therefore, impose sacrifice on a generation of faithful in view of a better Church tomorrow or at Omega Point.

Yet this is happening today: in the name of a shiny future (like the "next five-year plan" in Communist countries), the Church-intellectuals strike out in the direction of the hierarchy and the laity, sowing discord and distrust between them, and blackmailing both: first, to make them accept the "new Church," second, to make them doubt God's existence and providence. Let us be clear about it: each time a priest, or a nun, or a lay intellectual makes a blasphemous statement as is so current today, or fraternizes with the enemies of Christ, or deprives the Church of her splendor as Christ's bride, a blackmail is committed. For the faithful are ready for anything to keep their faith; they are willing to close an eye, even become blind to the provocations. One can almost hear their silent prayer that the provocation and the scandal might cease, that "progressive" pre-

lates and intellectuals might stop blaspheming, calling Christ
into question, demythologizing religion, and, worst of all,
talking about sex, sex, sex. As long as these prelates and intellectuals, showing off their newly-acquired miserable little erudition
(of Marx, Freud, Sartre) mocked with so much humor by Maritain in *Le Paysan de la Garonne,* and keep debating, analyzing,
scrutinizing with eyes fixed on their newspaper or television
"image," the misery of the faithful will grow and become
excruciating. Submerged under oceans of mud, unable to answer
and articulate his arguments, he is like Christ on the cross, the
cross of publicity. Not the Roman soldier's lance, but his own
priests' words wound his side and search his entrails.

A new, hard type of priest and ideologue is emerging in the
Church. They reject charity because they know love only in the
form of self-love and eager, jealous fulfillment of their potential
as rebels. Like all ideologues, they are impatient with human
beings who do not conform to the kind they approve and culti-
vate: either as cold as themselves—today's disciples, tomorrow's cadre—or manipulated and grateful pawns whose admiration is the only kind of sunshine they like to bask in.

Characteristic of these Church ideologues is their contemptuous rejection of the Church's past. Bultmann is not the only
one who demythologizes the first Christian centuries at the price
of calling the first Christians primitive, credulous, living in an
environment permeated by magic and miracle-makers. This is,
of course, a false picture, eagerly seized upon by credulous intellectuals ignorant of history. But then how can we believe them
when they loudly demand a return to the faith and style of the
first centuries? The demand is not genuine, for the whole demythologization of the Church's past is based on the modern
intellectual view of the "masses" and their supposed lack of
knowledge, experience, and sophistication, their mental distance from self-satisfied intellectuals. Ordinary people are, if
anything, less credulous than intellectuals. The history of
contemporary communism shows very well that only the latter,
not the "masses," were taken in by slogans, promises, and uto-

pian horizons; it is especially the educated, not the peasants and workers, who believed again and again that the Party would mellow, liberalize and democratize itself, and finally create paradise on earth.

There is no reason to believe that contemporaries of Herodotus, Caesar, Ovid, or Augustine had less (or more) common sense than people today. To speak of them as lesser lights than modern man is intended as a discreditation of Christianity and the consequent accreditation of the brilliant destiny of "man come of age." But it is rather obvious that men living much closer to nature than our city-bred, skeptical yet propaganda-fed urbanites, convinced themselves quite accurately before accepting something surprising, unexpected, or out of the ordinary. There were around Christ all kinds of people: fishermen, carpenters, rabbis, businessmen, Pharisees, prostitutes, Romans, Jews, Greeks, and Syrians. Yet versions hostile to him were only circulated much later, from understandably hostile Jewish sources concerning his illegitimate birth, fathered by the legionnaire Panther.

On the contrary, writes historian Marcel Bloch, founder, with Lucien Febvre, of the modern historical school in France,

> Christianity is a religion documented by history. Other religious systems could and did establish their beliefs and rites on a mythology external to human times. But the sacred books of the Christians are history books and their liturgy commemorates their God's life on earth. . . . No doubt, one can conceive a religious experience owing nothing to historical events. For the Deist, an internal illumination is enough to believe in God. Not so for belief in the Christian God. Because Christianity is, by its essence, a religion based on history which means that its principal dogmas rest on actual events. Read your Creed: "I believe in Jesus Christ . . . [who] suffered under Pontius Pilate . . . [and] the

third day he rose again from the dead." Here the beginnings
of the faith are seen also as its foundation.

There is also a third reason for the constant aggresstion on
the mental powers and reliability of the Gospel writers and their
sources. Christianity, and Christ Himself, were born among ordinary people of modest condition. The whole enterprise of the
Church-intellectuals, so immensely flattered that they may now
join their secularistic colleagues, is based on contempt for such
people called "masses" since Hegel and Marx, and despised by
the existentialists of Paris and New York. In the eyes of these
people Christ Himself appears as a *déclassé*, surrounded by
prostitutes, wastrels, publicans, beggars, and people with a de-
cidedly bad conscience. He is even hated by these cold ideologues and social planners since He encouraged waste in the
nonaffluent society of his friends. Did he not say to them who
cried out as Mary Magdalene was pouring myrrh on his feet:
"Let her alone. . . . you will always have the poor around you,
but you will not always have me." This kind of statement is
intolerable for the hard, efficient men and masculine women
among whom Church-intellectuals recruit members to their
caste.

Marxism and other such theories have sharpened this contempt to the point where it becomes class hatred. The nonintellectuals, laymen and priests, are treated with arrogance because they slow down the secularization process and the stream-
lining of the Church. Their crime is that they feel comfortable
among traditional forms, not only because these forms are old

9 *Métier d'historien*, ed. Armand Colin, 1949. This was also the theme,
namely the historicity of the Gospels, of Pope Paul's discourse at the general
audience of December 28, 1966. "Since we did not have the happiness of
knowing the Lord in a direct manner," the Pope said, "we should strive to
have a historical knowledge of Him. . . . Great discussions take place about
this matter today, provoked in minds seduced by study and interpretation,
and who would belittle the Gospels' historical value, particularly the parts
concerning Jesus' birth and childhood. . . . You must know how to defend,
through study and faith, the comforting certainty that the Gospels are not
an invention of popular imagination, but that they tell the truth." Note that
this discourse dealt with the first of the fashionable errors mentioned by
Cardinal Ottaviani's letter to the bishops of all nations.

and thus venerable, not only because they are beautiful, but also because things and people, after living together and sharing the same roof, feel happy in one another's company. Yet this the Church-intellectuals cannot accept for reasons so well-described by Mr. Michael Wharton:

> The theorists and dreamers of the scientific world have already realized that the drag in this process, the unassimilated factor, is humanity itself, physically inefficient, still clinging to all sorts of customs, attitudes, and desires which belong to the unscientific past, sometimes called the Childhood of the human Race.[10]

If the Church-intellectuals surround Teilhard de Chardin with a veritable cult, it is because he justifies their contempt for ordinary people and relieves them from the obligations of charity. Through his evolutionism he provides a "scientific" basis for their impatience with past forms and with people refusing to live in a world of change and flux. He preaches to them that science itself condemns the nonmodern, the undemocratic, the nonprogressive to die out so as not to obstruct mankind's cosmic adventure. While Engels and Trotsky merely consigned these nonconforming types to the "rubbish heap of history," Father Teilhard rejects them even more categorically by calling in Darwinism and sentencing them, as no longer useful social organs, to the rubbish heap of biology. The sinister Sister Aloysius puts it this way: "As long as we maintain patterns high in detail and fixity, we encourage people to join us who need a haven, the very people who won't be able to function in the sort of world taking shape under our eyes." [11]

Christ himself is chastised and recrucified in such a statement since he founded his Church in order to provide a haven for people who "do not function" according to the world's criteria of efficiency. But, of course, Sister Aloysius's Church is not that of Christ: it is a business organization of bureaucrat priests and hard-eyed, Sartre-quoting nuns, always eager to make a deal

[10] *Catholic Herald* (London), November 25, 1966.
[11] The already-quoted symposium in *Commonweal.*

with the powerful. It is somewhat out of proportion to quote Nietzsche at this point, but a passage in his *Untimely Considerations* pinpoints this obsession with success:

> Hegel inplanted into generations permeated by his doctrine the admiration for the "power of history" which easily becomes the naked admiration of success and the idolatry of facts. Well, people who have learned how to bend their backbone before the power of history, will mechanically approve any kind of power, that of government, public opinion, or majority. . . . We will have then the religion of the power of history and we will have priests genuflecting to "necessary ideas."

Georges Bernanos expressed this much more simply: the time will come, he wrote, when people like me will be shot by Bolshevik priests!

Christ knew these people, he referred to them as whited sepulchres, and placed them infinitely below sinners and publicans. Indeed, they do not possess the pagan's *joie de vivre*, nor the heart's and body's courage to sin *fortiter*. And they are not interested in profit like the publican, only in power. They are the spiritual brothers and sisters of the Nazi doctors and nurses who performed laboratory experiments on human beings. They too were products of the efficiency cult. Did not one of the symposium ladies in *Commonweal* recommend that women modify their biological nature in order to release their intellectual potential? Did Teilhard de Chardin not speak of the need to develop a "noble form of eugenics" if we want a more united and cooperating world where "there is no place for the poor in spirit, the skeptics, the pessimists, the sad of heart, the weary, and the immobilists?" He wanted to breed "a new type of men: scientists, thinkers, airmen," just like the Soviet biologists Michurin and Lysenko, Stalin's proteges, who claimed to satisfy the Communists' yearning for absolute power over life, the ability to erase the limits separating the species. It is again Bernanos' prophetic intuition which expresses admirably this temptation and this threat. He foresaw the time when "committees of psychologists will argue with committees of moralists and committees of theologians until the citizen's every last indefeasible right will be warranted by half a score of governmental offices, open daily from nine to five, excepting of course Sundays and holidays." [12] Theologians as part of the State apparatus and giving their expert opinion on how to deal with Teilhard's "weary and sad of heart": is this not the new breed Church-intellectuals' portrait?

The balance in Christendom can only be restored if the laity makes use of the reemphasized recognition of its role in the Church. When I say this, I am not guided by a desire to renew the medieval conciliar theory that councils, with laymen in attendance also, should have preeminence over the pope, nor am I guided by a false and romantic democratism. The laity must reassert the importance of common sense so as to give the papacy and the healthy part of the hierarchy the leverage they need in their conflict with the Church intellectuals. It is significant that in his eighty-fourth year, Jacques Maritain's presumably last book asserts the same point already in the title and subtitle: the "paysan de la Garonne" is a paraphrase of a French saying which denotes common sense with its genuine primitiveness in contact with the real world. While the subtitle: "an old layman's reflection on our times," means, as Maritain himself explains, that he wrote it as *un laic invétéré*, a convinced and hidebound layman. No wonder that the book is attacked viciously in France, particularly by those whom Maritain, himself a onetime Church-intellectual, has now disappointed with his return to good sense.

Laymen as such do not necessarily possess common sense at any appreciable degree, except in contrast to intellectuals blinded by the love of abstractions and blueprints. Love of abstractions is a luxury that nonintellectuals can hardly afford: physicians, merchants, manual workers, peasants, housewives, curates must take reality into account, otherwise they are at once penalized. In the case of teachers, journalists, fashionable priests, writers, and generally "idea men," there is the saving

[12] *Lettre aux Anglais*, p. 183. Editions des Cahiers du Témoignage Chrétien, 1942.

device of a wide margin between bad judgment or intellectual dishonesty, on the one hand, and life's revenge on the other. Nevertheless, it is said that the latter possess insights and, of course, culture, which sharpen the judgment and widen the perspective; whereas the former have their noses too near their work to develop a fair sense for comparisons and nuances. This view is obviously accredited by intellectuals, and is not based on reality. The so-called ordinary man has rather fewer than more numerous artificial needs, and the needs he does have are not veiled from his eyes, like from the eyes of intellectuals, by a kind of second ego, compounded of snobbishness and a cultural self-image. The ordinary man's spiritual needs arise directly from the necessities of life, simply because he allows his natural responses to guide him, whereas the intellectual tends to suppress his spir-itual needs as if they were shameful unless analyzed. But when these needs are analyzed, they are most probably explained away or reduced to something unrecognizable and unspiritual. As Kierkegaard says so well (in *Post-Scriptum*) of the relationship between philosophers (intellectuals) and Christian faith, they trust their own speculative ability to transform into "real truth" that which is only "relative truth" in the minds of simple believ-ers. But is it not precisely the thinker's privilege, asks Kierke-gaard, to understand better the faith in its simplicity, rather than to intellectualize it until it evaporates?

When we ask ourselves whether there was a need for the complex event described as updating the Church, we may only answer modestly that the calling together of a Council is a chap-ter in Church history that no individual should judge, approve, or condemn merely by his own lights. Indirectly, however, we may conclude that while the term *aggiornamento* does not have a clear meaning, the Council, as an examination of the state of the Church, was a good thing: it permitted to bring out into the open the insufficiencies of which the Church must have suffered for a long time if we judge by what has been revealed in the past few years. The priests and nuns and Church-intellectuals who behave now disgracefully must have been merely quiet but not less disgraceful in their hearts during the past decades. And certain documents circulated during the council sessions listed revolutionary demands going far beyond even that which we find intolerably scandalous.

The immediate and most important consequences of these scandals are internal disaffection and the concomitant drop in the number of conversions. The Church is a reverential society which, as Pope Paul said, cannot and will not accept a democratization of its structure. But reverence is not merely a superficial matter of observing the rules and roles of hierarchic structure, it is the recognition of another's spiritual superiority, itself received from the divinity of Christ. Every act of callousness, frivolousness, or mundanity in priests and nuns represents a diminution of reverence, a decrease and weakening of vocations, the spread of cynical indifference throughout the body of the Church, and increasing consternation among hopeful converts.[13]

The latter suffer perhaps most. They become Catholics out of various, to others mostly unknown motives, but the basic ones are evident: they want to find a solid ground under their feet and the grace of God above their head. No amount of psychosocial analysis can alter this. But many converts or prospective converts are asking now, why should they join the Church when they find there the same mundane concerns as outside, perhaps with a touch of hypocrisy and clumsiness added? Similarly, why should a young Catholic girl wish to become a nun when nuns now attend charm courses like airline stewardesses, and their menus in the convents are discussed on the food section pages of ladies' journals? The irony is that this is done in the name of "opening the windows onto the modern world" when in reality it is a crude imitation of seventeenth-century abesses and prioresses with their mundane way of life and coquettishness. But when a modern girl aspires to the pleasures of the world is it not more logical for her to become a stewardess, a secretary, or a

[13] The percentage of converts to Catholicism in the United States is steadily dropping in proportion to population growth. According to figures published in *America* (Aug. 6, 1966), in 1956 there were 139.333 converts out of a population of 167 million; in 1966 only 123.149 converts out of a population of 195 million.

housewife? Why should she choose a convent? Similarly, why should a Catholic boy becomes a priest when so many better opportunities exist in the world to run a social welfare agency or a business enterprise? [14]

To these questions Father Karl Rahner has given his answer. "Why should we, Catholics, be worried if we are only 17 per cent of the world's population. Just where is it written that *we* must have the whole 100 per cent? God must have all. But we cannot say that he is doing so only if we, meaning the Church, have everybody." We answer Rahner that it was Christ who said that we must strive to have 100 per cent through teaching, converting, and setting example. Not by reorganizing society which, as Gustave Thibon points out, is "a convenient alibi of modern Messianism," [15] but by the hard business of individual conversions. And individuals will respond by seeking conversion even in this hard world of ours, although not to the loud statements of hard-eyed priests or mundane nuns, but only to the Good Message: Christ is born to save you.

[14] Father Andrew Greeley pointed out (*The Sign*, November 1966) the crisis in vocations and defections. He speaks of a "vanishing priesthood" as a distinct possibility. Father Greeley does not hide that the root of this problem is an "identity crisis" among Catholics, and that the identity crisis was created by "the drumfire of criticism in the Catholic liberal press." As a result, priests and religious, Greeley writes, "are not sure whether they have not wasted their lives."

[15] *Back to Reality*, p. 81. Hollis and Carter, London, 1955.

VIII

CONCLUSION:
THE PROSPECTS

I have written in this book about dialogue, updating, communism, the communications media—things new in history and in the history of the Church. Throughout, however, I insisted also on the fact that in their essential aspects they are not new at all; while dialoguers, updaters, or sympathizers with totalitarian ideologies consider themselves revolutionary innovators, the Church, in her wisdom and permanence knows them for what they are: new-breed formulators of old errors, children and grandchildren of the Tempter.

The Church knows them because they are the old idol worshipers in new-breed garb. Too impatient and proud to accept the absolute as transcendental yet personal, they seek it in some earthly embodiment, powerful enough to appear like an absolute, yet in need of interpreters and manipulators. The absolute is henceforth called History, Evolution, Technology, Mature Mankind, Omniscient State, or something else. The essential thing is that it should be visible, palpable, manipulable.

The world which seeks the absolute in one of these incarnations is exactly the de-Christianized milieu of which Maritain and Guardini, among others, have written. They warned that the time would come and that Christians will have all the difficulty adjusting to it, surviving in it. This generation sees better perhaps than these writers why adjustment is more than just difficult. Maritain meant by desacralization that the world will abandon its central inspiration, the truth of religion. It is questionable whether he foresaw that all values, closely or remotely dependent on this truth, will also be discarded with a sudden and violent shock, and that a centrifugal force will scatter them until they cease to be operative in our lives. With the same speed, the earthly embodiments of the absolute also follow one another: everyday a new absolute is discovered, so that only the most brutal ones remain eventually imposed.

In this situation the Christian is supposed to hold onto his truth, presumably not like a new catacomb-dweller, although that is exactly what he is forced to do under Communist regimes, but like a lonely man who is, however, encouraged and supported by the Roman Church. After all, the desacralized world predicted by trustworthy Catholic writers was to be democratic, pluralistic; why should the Catholic Church not have full license to perform her task in it, to aid Christians in their religious life? The question is, of course, rhetorical. The point is that the de-Christianized world is not merely indifferent to Catholicism, not even merely hostile to it; it is a world expressly designed by antispiritual, anti-Christian forces, it is the secular city, the non-Church. It clashes on an increasing number of points with religion, so that Maritain's injunction, that Catholics should bring their full cooperation to the shaping of the new world, reveals itself increasingly impossible. It is no longer a question of holding onto a few dogmas—the essentials—and letting go the worldview attached to these dogmas as inessential.

The Christian may find solace in what Father Jean Danielou wrote recently of the necessity to Christianize the milieu in which we live. This suggestion is contrary to Maritain's thesis, and it looks the problem squarely in the face. Its precise meaning is that it is not enough to hold onto dogmas only as if the Christian were an orphan, happy to be alive although deprived of a home; dogmas must have a radiation through which they permeate civilization. It would be an artificial world in which civilization would be counted among the inessentials. And civilization does not consist of the daily repetition of prayers or proclamations of doctrinal truths, it is not a breviary for the reading of which one sets aside a special hour. Civilization consists of daily acts, including the hardly conscious ones which constitute the fabric of existence which distinguish a man from a brute, a better man from a worse man.

The argument that Catholics may give up the inessentials provided they keep the doctrine and the faith is the most dangerous argument of all. The Tempter in his distorted wisdom knows this well; he knows that he cannot attack the central fortress without previously preparing the terrain leading to it. He never tells the Christian: Give up your faith! Do not believe in Christ! Question the Creed! His work is the slow erosion of Christian civilization, a huge yet fragile domain. While people look at him fascinated and unwary, he advances, at first alone and on tiptoe; then at the head of a marching and drumbeating battalion. By the time we wake up they have reached the fortress. And this was made possible because we have been retreating from one "inessential" to the next.

This is not a metaphysical description, it is the concrete description of how things happen. Even the role of the Church-intellectuals can be clearly pinpointed in the process: they are the ones who replace one "inessential" with another "inessential," gradually until the whole fabric of civilization is transformed beyond recognition. In our century the Church-intellectuals admire Marxism, and *through Marxism* the industrial efficiency, particularly its power. We witness the transformation of Christian civilization into Marxist civilization, or, if you prefer, into a materialistic, secular, collectivistic, and merciless civilization.

The crowning task of the Church-intellectual has been the introduction of this civilization into the fortress, the Church.

When Lenin said that religion must not be, cannot be destroyed by a frontal attack, only by disintegration from within, he did not only draw a blueprint of operation for his Party, he foresaw what was to happen in the world at large. He foresaw what we see today: that the Church-intellectuals remain in the Church, although most of them can hardly be called Christians. The Pope stated recently,

> We know, unfortunately, that nowadays certain trends of thought *which still describe themselves as Catholic* attempt to attribute a priority in the normative formulation of the truth of the Faith to the community of the faithful . . . and not to the teaching authority of the one who occupies the chair of Peter.

"Still describe themselves as Catholic"—the subject of this half-sentence could be many things and many people. Why, indeed, do the Church-intellectuals remain in the Church when they have ceased to belong to it in spirit and obedience? Two reasons emerged during our discussion in this book: the temptation for some repressed energies to plunge into the middle of things, to be advertised as intellectual vanguard. When a Father Rahner belittles "folklore religiosity" and speaks the language of the "atomic age," he thinks he espouses the spirit of the time, that of efficiency; when the Abbé Oraison declares that "Christ transcended the genital form of religiousness," he knows he intrigues all and sundry, and creates in pious minds a minuscule mental orgy; when the World Council of Churches recommends revolutionary violence and extramarital sex as factors of social change, its members feel power swelling in their breast as co-directors of tomorrow's world.[1]

And so on. Now this coveted vanguard role is linked to the sacerdotal status; Rahner, Oraison, Fathers Dubay or Curran would not even stir a teacup storm if they were outside the Ecclesia.

The second reason is that these men genuinely want to

[1] Cf. Conference on Church and Society held by the World Council of Churches in Geneva, July 1966.

change the Church, to streamline and modernize it, to make it less "divisive" in a world which they erroneously see as transformed, coalesced, fraternal, jubilantly cooperating for cosmic adventures. They would agree with Doctor Outler, the Methodist bishop, who foresees, within a decade, "a plurality of Churches in full communion, with diverse rites and institutional organizations, truly one in Christ as one Church, but multiform —truly Catholic, evangelical and reformed." [2]

This image is not modeled on the *Decree of Ecumenism* that I quoted in another chapter, but on the ephemeral pattern of the pluralistic society, the United Nations, and other organizations which preach unity while practicing the opposite. So that disappointment is bound to come sooner or later to the new-breed Church-intellectual. Since his reformism bears so obviously the mark of the time and of a certain form of civilization, as this form vanishes and yields to another, the ground of his reformism will be pulled out from under him. This will be followed by more realism on the part of some, but also by more impatience on the part of others. At any rate, it is likely that the Church's self-styled reformers will turn into genuine schismatics, although, let us hope, only a fraction of today's loud agitators will choose this path. I think we will then witness a psychological evolution similar to that of great schismatics of former times: pride, an always growing pride, will finally force the truly radical ones among the new breed to break with the Church and leave her. Partly because success will have spoiled them (their reformism, outlandish as it is, is at this early date already congealing into an establishment in its own right), partly because progress, in their estimation, can never be fast enough.

If I am asked, in conclusion, what are the prospects for the Church at the end of her crisis: slow Protestantization or the restoration of true doctrine and humility, I answer with the words of Christ: "I am with you always until the end of the world," again, "I will build My Church, and the forces of Death's realm shall not subdue it."

[2] "Reformation Roman Style," *The Catholic World*, March 1967.

INDEX